MEET IT

Iceberg of Deception - A Look Beneath the Surface

RICK HOWARD

Remnant Publications

Printed in the USA

Published by Remnant Publications, Inc.
649 E. Chicago Road
Coldwater, MI 49036
517-279-1304
www.remnantpublications.com

The author assumes full responsibility for the accuracy of all facts and quotations as cited in this book.

Unless otherwise noted, Scripture quotations are taken from The Holy Bible, King James Version.

Cover designed by David Berthiaume
Text designed by Greg Solie • Altamont Graphics

ISBN: 978-1-629130-11-8
RP1145

Table *of* Contents

Dedication

To the many people sensitive to God's guidance, who encouraged me and helped me to research this project.

To Rosalie, who has stood by my side for forty-six years and who willingly parsed through some of these weighty aspects with me.

To our children, Jason, Jen, Brian, Jessica and Stacy for their loving support, friendship and wise counsel.

All of these wonderful people have bolstered me with prayer and patience and with their expressions of love and encouragement, both spoken and implied.

And finally and foremost, to Jesus, Who lovingly leads me forward, sustaining me to approach these most sensitive matters that test the veracity and very purpose of His church.

Purpose

The purpose of this book is to address a fast-paced, influential movement that is advancing within the Seventh-day Adventist Church, especially for the purposes of understanding and verifying its credibility and trustworthiness.

This book is not meant to stop something but to start something. It is meant to engage your inquiry, examination, and evaluation of the influence of emerging church theology and its vehicles. Deserving of scrutiny, just as is this book, the question must be answered: is emerging church theology a threat to God's beloved church? If so, is it a mystic kiss blown upon us by Satan's corrupt hand, or has it been promulgated among us by well-intentioned people? To form a determination, we must know what it is—its origin, its action, and its impact. For the purposes of discernment and recognition, we must discover the "*who*" and "*where*" of it. The intention of the author is to search these things together.

Inspiration claims that the "omega" deception evolves; it is "a train of heresies," not just one, all of which are a part of the end-time omega. This amorphous creature may now be threatening the church, and we will investigate how serious of a threat it may be.

A Note *from the* Author

I certainly thought and prayed about how to serve God after retirement, but, as is so often the case, He leads where we had not intended to go. Near the end of fifteen years as pastor of the Hilton Head and Beaufort Seventh-day Adventist Churches within the Carolina Conference, I began realizing that a seed of thought was growing—one I had to recognize, respect, and finally heed. There was just too much prodding, evidence, and providence confirming that I needed to write about a specific topic—a work I never, ever would have undertaken without God's continual guidance and encouragement. Why? Because I am not a writer.

In retrospect, I can see how God led, gently urging my head elder to find a way to whisper in my ear, "Rick, you must write a book about this." For ten years, Elder Ken Holland patiently planted that seed. He had spent his life in the publishing work, for a time as editor of *These Times* magazine and *Signs of the Times*, preceding their present editor, Marvin Moore. His burden for the written word and its service to the church and Lord he dearly loved was clear. As my head elder, Ken did not know of my struggle as he, on those occasions I spoke on the subject of spiritualistic inclinations threatening our church, spurred me on to write. I realized God had imparted to me a unique understanding as a result of my experiences before becoming a Christian, experiences through which He led and delivered. I had been convicted to share that perspective over the years; however, I knew that conviction does not a writer make—at all! Neither did my past technical writing in chemistry. In fact, it was more of a hindrance. I shrank from the responsibility for ten years. But as always, His leading and timing are perfect.

The Hilton Head Seventh-day Adventist Church lost Ken's wise leadership when he passed away on his 89th birthday. With the passing of time, observing the subtle increase of spiritualistic practices in the church, I grew more concerned. Then, about a year later, while praying alone in my church office, I suddenly and distinctly heard the words in my mind that

Ken used to speak to me, "Rick, you must write a book about all this." It was startling, and I knew it was the Lord bringing Ken's words back to my mind in His unique way. I also knew that I was actually being led by the King of the Universe to write that book. Immediately, I began my research, knowing I should wait no longer.

Within an hour, two couples walked into church, enjoying its unique, simple beauty. On their way to California from London, their plane had been held over in Savannah, and they had decided to rent a car to spend the day sightseeing. Without searching, they found themselves in front of the Hilton Head Island Seventh-day Adventist Church and came in. They asked to take some pictures and I somewhat quickly toured them through the church, anxious to get back to my new project. I told them I was heading back to my office should they need anything, and left them to wander about. It wasn't long before I looked up at one of the women standing in my doorway, staring at the heap of books and papers that now covered my desk. It was a mess, and I was somewhat embarrassed. She asked what had me so involved and I found myself recounting the entire story all the way up to what had taken place that morning, finishing with that I believed the Lord was leading me to write. When I finally finished, she asked, "What will the book be about?" I didn't believe she would be aware of the subject and said, "The alpha and omega." Excitedly she said, "Oh, we need a book about that," and reached out her hand to shake mine, while introducing herself as the vice president of Pacific Press. She went on to tell me of their valued friendship with the Hollands and spent the next hour kindly giving me instructions on writing a book. She marveled at how God had led them that morning, having never been in the area before; He had led them on that day, on the very morning after ten years of the Lord's gentle leading. She marveled, as did I.

Gratefully, His amazing providences did not stop there, but in fact grew. He continues to lead with every forward advance in exposing the alpha and the omega. That book was *The Omega Rebellion*, which exposes the origins and dangers of a relatively new spiritual discipline: spiritual formation, its methods, and its threats. Since the omega is a train of heresies, *Meet It* moves on to expose specific movements impacting our church, tracking their origins and development.

I would ask that you kindly consider a few points:

Style versus content: Personal writing style, while susceptible to criticism, could result in reactive conclusions that will not lead anyone to discern truth. Proof through Scripture and the Spirit of Prophecy will. It seems fundamental and obvious, but reactive thinking can happen quickly, even if negligible, and can yield an outcome that is false or superficial at best. Requiring dedication to Scripture, the Spirit of Prophecy, along with a conviction of our mission, the researcher must be willing to accept Inspiration in its true context, dealing honestly with what is discovered. We will find all of the needed principles in Scripture and the specific application of those principles in the Spirit of Prophecy.

Safety versus controversy: While some matters by nature cause distress and even division, inviting criticism and disapproval, they must be taken into account. Measuring and testing the teachings of our church in the present day can insinuate an unloving quality in our atmosphere, creating an impression that is not at all Jesus-centric. But it is imperative that we stop, maybe often, and remember that each teaching, each doctrine, is borne out of Christ's love, that each directs us to His cross and can be successfully tried through Him.

In addition, whatever controversy must be reconciled through the years, it is present in our church in concert with God's will and plan; He is leading us through to glory.

Again, prove points in this book right or wrong with Inspiration; and consider, if they are found to be correct, what then?

Foreword

By Steve Wohlberg

"To everything there is a season," wrote King Solomon. "A time for every purpose under heaven" (Ecclesiastes 3:1, NKJV). Among the various times listed, there is not only "a time to keep silence," but also "a time to speak" (verse 7). In his newest book *Meet It*, which is a sequel to his former book *The Omega Rebellion*, Pastor Rick Howard boldly speaks out against emerging church heresies and Roman Catholic mysticism, which is not outside Adventism but within it.

In 1989, two years before I was ordained in the Dakota Conference, I had a memorable visit with then Mid-America Union President Joel Tompkins. We discussed the Desmond Ford crisis of the 1970s and early 1980s, which resulted in many Adventists, including pastors, abandoning our church. "When that crisis was growing," Elder Tompkins reflected solemnly, "the big guns [meaning many of our own leaders] were silent. When I saw the fallout, I vowed to God that if I ever saw something dangerous like that creeping into our church again, I would blow the trumpet."

I have never forgotten those words.

Now, don't miss this point: what made the Ford crisis so subtle and deadly was that Dr. Ford worked to destroy our prophetic message in the name of Jesus Christ. Verbally, he exalted Jesus, yet at the same time attacked Daniel 8:14, "the central pillar of the advent faith" (*The Great Controversy*, 409). Study that history; these are facts.

If you think about it, defenders of Sunday observance do essentially the same thing: they reject the Bible Sabbath under the guise of honoring Jesus Christ's resurrection. When the mark of the beast hits, something similar will occur again. The papal Sunday will be enforced by those claiming to serve our Savior. Paul's warning to the Corinthians about mistakenly following "another Jesus" (see 2 Corinthians 11:4) forcefully applies in each case.

There is no doubt that our beloved Seventh-day Adventist Church is facing another crisis much bigger than that which rocked Adventism in the

1970s and 1980s. Whether or not you discern this crisis and its cunning deceptions, the peril is real and souls are in danger. In a nutshell, the battle is over who is the real Jesus, how we can experience His true presence, what His real gospel is, and the meaning of obedience to His law by His grace. Open the Bible and read for yourself. Jesus Christ gave us His book of Revelation (see Revelation 1:1), His three angels' messages (Revelation 14:6–12), and the writings of His servant Ellen White: for "the testimony of Jesus is the spirit of prophecy" (Revelation 19:10).

Every Adventist needs this Jesus to be supreme—our all.

Some think we must reinvent Adventism to reach our youth. Apparently, the pure gospel of Jesus Christ, the holy truth, and the three angels' messages isn't enough. They think we need louder music, not hymns; more "conversation," less doctrine; and even "new experiences" guided by Roman Catholic mystics. Essentially, they think we need an emerging church type of revival, which is why some among us have been inviting emerging church mystics like Brian McLaren and Leonard Sweet to speak to our leaders, pastors, and youth.

Think about this. In the early 1900s, through John Harvey Kellogg's mystical book *The Living Temple*, Satan slithered right into our church to deceive Seventh-day Adventists. Even "the Lord's institution" and "our publishing house" were infected. Lucifer attacked, but Jesus Christ countered through His messenger. In 1901, Ellen White wrote:

> I feel a terror of soul as I see to what a pass our publishing house has come. The presses in the Lord's institution have been printing *the soul-destroying theories of Romanism and other mysteries of iniquity.* The office must be purged of this objectionable matter (*Testimonies for the Church*, vol. 8, 91, emphasis added).

She then warned specifically about Dr. Kellogg's book:

> In the book *Living Temple* there is presented the alpha of deadly heresies. The omega will follow, and will be received by those who are not willing to heed the warning God has given (*Selected Messages*, book 1, 200).

> I am instructed to speak plainly. "Meet it," is the word spoken to me. "Meet it firmly, and without delay" (Ibid.).

The time to *Meet It* is now.

Here's another sequence of events that I believe is worth sharing. In the spring of 2013, I was contacted by Generation of Youth for Christ Southeast (GYCSE), and the individual informed me that they were looking for a speaker for their October 9–12 conference at Southern Adventist University (SAU). GYCSE was looking for someone to "refute and present against the emerging church and spiritual formation." These GYCSE young people were deeply concerned about how Catholic mysticism has been invading Adventism.

On Sabbath morning, October 12, 2013, I delivered my address, titled "Perils of the Emerging Church," in the gymnasium of SAU. Honestly, I didn't expect what happened next. "Your talk is #1 on Audio Verse," beeped a text message on my cell phone.

I checked, and it was true. Five weeks later, it had been downloaded more than 30,000 times. Then ADvindicate.com interviewed me for more details, and last I checked, their article resulted in more than 2,000 "shares" to readers' Facebook pages. This was easily topped by a November 22 ADvindicate posting of an official statement from SAU's School of Religion faculty expressing emerging church concerns. In only four days, that latter article garnered more than 6,500 Facebook shares.

I mention these details to demonstrate that large numbers of Seventh-day Adventists, youth included (remember, GYC is largely run by young people), are highly interested in this topic and in avoiding emerging church delusions. More and more, God's people are waking up to the spiritual significance of this controversy raging among us. His saints are aroused.

Truly, the climate is ripe for *Meet It*.

Its time is now.

Moving beyond *The Omega Rebellion*, *Meet It* dives even deeper beneath the surface and shows exactly how emerging church errors, ecumenical pitfalls, occult techniques, New Age notions, pantheistic philosophy, and Roman Catholic mysticism have ever-so-slyly entered Adventism in the name of Jesus under the guise of promoting a closer "experience" with God. To the unwary, such ideas sound grand. However, below the surface, they are actually part of a brilliantly laid satanic plot to overthrow our fundamental mission and message. They're spiritual poison, especially to our youth, who lack experience and often fail to detect these errors.

"Protestantism," which surely applies to some Adventists too, "shall stretch her hand across the gulf to grasp the hand of the Roman power." Worse still, "she shall reach over the abyss to clasp hands with Spiritualism"

(*Testimonies for the Church*, vol. 5, 451). "All the world wondered after the beast," saith the Lord (see Revelation 13:3).

Dear reader, the beast is still the beast.

Pastor Rick Howard has 35 years of experience as a Seventh-day Adventist minister, and he has served as a pastor of both small and large congregations. Prior to his becoming a Seventh-day Adventist, he spent five years searching for truth within the maze of occult philosophy before he was miraculously rescued by the grace of Jesus Christ. Pastor Rick knows the facts about occultism and spiritualism. He sincerely cares about God's people, too much to keep silent.

Notice carefully what else the real Jesus said through His servant:

> The enemy is preparing for his last campaign against the church ... and when he makes another advance move, [many] will not recognize him as their enemy, that old serpent. (*Testimonies for the Church*, vol. 5, 294)

> The church may appear as about to fall, but it does not fall. It remains, while the sinners in Zion will be sifted out—the chaff separated from the precious wheat. This is a terrible ordeal, but nevertheless it must take place. (*Selected Messages*, book 2, 380)

> To stand in defense of truth and righteousness when the majority forsake us, to fight the battles of the Lord when champions are few—this will be our test. (*Testimonies for the Church*, vol. 5, 136, emphasis added)

On July 3, 2010, at the 59th Session of the General Conference of Seventh-day Adventists in Atlanta, Georgia, President Ted Wilson urged all Adventists to:

> Stay away from non-biblical spiritual disciplines or methods of spiritual formation that are rooted in mysticism such as contemplative prayer, centering prayer, and the emerging church movement in which they are promoted.

In *Meet It*, as in *The Omega Rebellion*, Pastor Rick Howard echoes Elder Wilson's exact concerns. Ultimately, Pastor Howard's deepest passion is the salvation of souls. By God's grace, he wants all of us to join him inside the glittering gates of the New Jerusalem instead of being outside "in the lake which burns with fire and brimstone," experiencing the unspeakable horror of "the second death" (see Revelation 21:8).

To all the readers of this book I say, Jesus loves us. He hung on a cruel cross for our sins, and then He rose from the dead. If any of us has been seduced by Satan's science without realizing it, rest assured that if we discover our error, repent, and trust our Savior, He will forgive, heal, and give us a true experience with God. But full submission is required, not only to His love and grace but also to His Word and counsel.

According to God's messenger, "the alpha of deadly heresies" is behind us. Yet "the omega would follow" and would "be received by those who are not willing to heed the warning God has given." Is "the omega" upon us? If so, then the final "shaking" of Adventism is at the door.

Reading Rick Howard's book *Meet It* will help protect you and your loved ones from subtle delusions lurking within emerging church teachings.

As Elder Joel Tompkins testified, there is a time to blow the trumpet.

Introduction

Overview

Satan plans to usher the celebrating and infatuating world of his fallen churches into God's remnant church by charming whomever he can with the belief that if they will only join with them in their emerging culture, then the Seventh-day Adventist Church will have finally arrived, and we will be accepted as equals. Thus, he plans to destroy God's church.

To be recognized as an equal by the sisterhood of Protestant churches is extremely desirable to those in our church who are tired of being looked at as a "peculiar people" (Titus 2:14). For 150 years, we have believed that those churches from which some in our church want acceptance are what constitute "fallen Christianity," Babylon and her daughters. God calls His people to come out of Babylon (see Revelation 18:4). However, it is with those churches that constitute Babylon that many in God's church now want to hold hands.

Satan will provoke as many as he can to ignore sensibility and to eventually despise the writings of Ellen White. He will do whatever he can to obstruct their use for guidance and for the drawing of God's people into a loving and saving relationship with their Creator; he is well aware that when the Spirit of Prophecy counsel is heeded, he loses—always.

As Satan undermines the legitimacy of the Spirit of Prophecy, he entices Adventists to crave repeatedly the more provocative practices he has introduced into his churches through the teachings of the emerging church. He then breaks down the doctrinal barriers that separate the churches, appealing to the sensibility of learning at his feet, in his churches and schools. He discerns that their freely-made decision to ignore God-given counsel "to refuse to even listen to those who mix truth with error" renders them within his jurisdiction (*Early Writings*, 124). The angels, who respect and love God's fundamental precept of freedom of choice, must back away, surrendering their provision of protection; and their evil counterparts stand ready to impart their machinations.

The discipline of spiritual formation was successfully crafted, employing the thirteen spiritual exercises supernaturally revealed to the founder of the Jesuits, Ignatius Loyola. This Ignatian spirituality specifically uses the mysticism within these exercises and makes way for the practice of contemplative prayer, which can also be referred to as centering prayer, breath prayer, or a variety of other names.

The innovative and current application of this deception from Roman Catholicism has been grandly ushered into today's Protestant churches and is intended to bring them under the Catholic Church's control. The vehicle for carrying these teachings to the Protestant churches is called the emerging church movement. This movement of Jesuit origins is meant to fulfill what has always been the sole purpose of the Jesuit order: to work toward bringing the world under the authority of the pope, who, for the first time in the history of the world is himself a practicing Jesuit. The new pope, Francis, advocates the teachings of spiritual formation and its mystical practices, all under the umbrella of Ignatian spirituality, which he constantly promotes.

This is no small thing! In sermon after sermon and in numerous articles, the new pope makes the claim that this type of spiritualism must be practiced to advance in the spiritual life. This type of spiritualism lies within the teachings of the emerging church movement, which also endorses a culture and philosophy meant to appeal to the postmodern minds of youth, which is the reason it is spreading so rapidly through colleges and universities.

Given their great success in the battle with Protestants during the Counter-Reformation in Europe, the Jesuits discern clearly that targeting the youth, the future leaders, is basic to the change of nations and religious thought. This time in life of newfound freedom coupled with the challenge to think independently makes way for the moralistic restructuring needed to rethink the role of religious doctrine. The emerging church movement, with its Jesuit-influenced thinking, is using these same methods, working feverishly to break down the barriers that exist between Protestant denominations to make way for one great movement. The most challenging but crucial barrier preventing a merger is that of the teaching and preaching of doctrine, the element that establishes individual denominations and is why downplaying doctrine is in the bull's-eye of the emerging church movement.

Inspiration teaches that the order of the Jesuits was founded to reestablish papal power in the world. Five hundred years ago, they fashioned a philosophy to regain that power. Should we take for granted the assumption that they are not adopting it today for the same purpose? Definitely not! It is worth reading a portion of the inspired statement from the Spirit of Prophecy that speaks to their plan to win youth through worship:

> They established colleges for the sons of princes and nobles, and schools for the common people; and the children of Protestant parents were drawn into an observance of popish rites. All the outward pomp and display of the Romish worship was brought to bear to confuse the mind, and dazzle and captivate the imagination; and thus the liberty for which the fathers had toiled and bled was betrayed by the sons. The Jesuits rapidly spread themselves over Europe, and wherever they went, there followed a revival of popery." (*The Great Controversy*, 1888 ed., 234)

As stated, "All the outward pomp and display of the Romish worship was brought to bear to confuse the mind, and dazzle and captivate the imagination." Today, this concept speaks to the state-of-the-art worship style of the emerging church, liberated and set free from the encumbered, even crippling, manner hampered by doctrine today and even back during the Counter-Reformation; it will surely "dazzle and captivate the imagination."

In later chapters of this book, we will examine a movement within God's church known as The One Project. Founded by well-intentioned Seventh-day Adventist pastors, the influence and impact of their chosen mode of study, George Fox University—known for its spiritualistic and emerging church teachings—is becoming increasingly and clearly exhibited.

We must not forget that Ignatian spirituality, spiritual formation, and contemplative spirituality are all methods planned by the Roman Catholic Church to win the entire world to their worship communion. "Religious institutes of the contemplative and of the active life, have so far played, and still do play, the main role in the evangelization of the world." [1]

To re-digest, the Roman Catholic Church, the beast power of Revelation chapter 13, plans to take control of the nations of this world, then all false religions of this world, and finally God's true church. Our mission and

1 Decree *Ad Gentes* on the Mission Activity of the Church, Vatican II, http://www.vatican.va/archive/hist_councils/ii_vatican_council/documents/vat-ii_decree_19651207_ad-gentes_en.html; (accessed February 10, 2014).

reason for existing is to call God's people out of Babylon and into His remnant church. To succeed, we must avoid the trap that Satan has set for the church throughout history—prevailing upon God's church to merge and interweave with the fallen Protestant churches of Babylon.

While we will enjoy the company of many of its members for eternity, going beyond the loving relationship demonstrated in the message of the three angels renders our beautiful truths diluted and often of none effect. Loving them and yearning for their salvation does not call for us to accept and teach their erroneous beliefs. Worship is also a legitimate concern, for we are warned not to "go to listen to error, without being obliged to go" (*Early Writings*, 124). Doing these things is evidence that we may have fallen into a satanic trap; the trap that has always been his most successful at stifling the message and outreach of God's people.

There are precious lessons to learn from history, especially those learned from Solomon's interaction with the world in his day. Let's look at few paragraphs from *Prophets and Kings* that describe those experiences.

Solomon's Fall—Why?

> In seeking to strengthen his relations with the powerful kingdom lying to the southward of Israel, Solomon ventured upon forbidden ground. Satan knew the results that would attend obedience; and during the earlier years of Solomon's reign—years glorious because of the wisdom, the beneficence, and the uprightness of the king—he sought to bring in influences that would insidiously undermine Solomon's loyalty to principle and cause him to separate from God. That the enemy was successful in this effort, we know from the record: "Solomon made affinity [likeness, fellow feeling, similarity] with Pharaoh king of Egypt, and took Pharaoh's daughter [acted on his feelings and desires, ignoring God's counsel], and brought her into the City of David." 1 Kings 3:1
>
> From a human point of view, this marriage, though contrary to the teachings of God's law, seemed to prove a blessing; for Solomon's heathen wife was converted and united with him in the worship of the true God. Furthermore, Pharaoh rendered signal service to Israel by taking Gezer, slaying "the Canaanites that dwelt in the

> city," and giving it "for a present unto his daughter, Solomon's wife." 1 Kings 9:16. This city Solomon rebuilt and thus apparently greatly strengthened his kingdom along the Mediterranean seacoast. But in forming an alliance with a heathen nation, and sealing the compact by marriage with an idolatrous princess, Solomon rashly disregarded the wise provision that God had made for maintaining the purity of His people. The hope that his Egyptian wife might be converted was but a feeble excuse for the sin....
>
> Solomon flattered himself that his wisdom and the power of his example would lead his wives from idolatry to the worship of the true God, and also that the alliances thus formed would draw the nations round about into close touch with Israel. Vain hope! Solomon's mistake in regarding himself as strong enough to resist the influence of heathen associates was fatal. And fatal, too, the deception that led him to hope that notwithstanding a disregard of God's law on his part, others might be led to revere and obey its sacred precepts. ...
>
> "The king made silver and gold at Jerusalem as plenteous as stones, and cedar trees made he as the sycamore trees that are in the vale for abundance." 2 Chronicles 1:15. Wealth, with all its attendant temptations, came in Solomon's day to an increasingly large number of people; but the fine gold of character was dimmed and marred. (*Prophets and Kings*, 53–55)

Solomon "flattered himself" and was no doubt flattered by the leaders of the surrounding nations. He believed his efforts were succeeding but they were not. Because of Solomon's refusal to follow God's counsel, Satan had the right to take control of all that was happening. Solomon was not aware that he changed leaders and was deceived by the excitement and the illusion of progress and success. The Lord's guiding and protective angels had to step aside and were no longer in control. Slowly, Solomon drifted away from God.

It may appear as if current practices of joining with the evangelical churches and the emerging church movement are bringing success, as Solomon believed. Nevertheless, we are counseled against this kind of relationship, and the results of disobedience are certain: apostasy. "I was shown the necessity of those who believe that we are having the last message of mercy, *being separate from those who are daily imbibing new errors* (*Early Writings*, 124, emphasis added)."

Are we attempting to use the same strategy as Solomon? Do we believe that while we ignore God's counsel we can win those in the fallen churches and bring revival to our own? We have been called of God to give the three angels' messages. But have some of us purposefully ignored God's instructions on how to evangelize the world. Are we using emerging church plans as a substitute?

We will attempt to answer these questions (and more) in *Meet It,* a book whose title is taken from a dream God gave His messenger more than 100 years ago: a dream instructing the church on how to confront a similar danger, which she called the "alpha of a train of heresies," that threatened the church at that time. Whether the danger exposed in this book is the omega of that "train of heresies" or not, it needs to be exposed as a movement that may be leading our youth and others onto dangerous ground.

Chapter One:

The Great Controversy Theme

The heart and soul of the Seventh-day Adventist Church is rooted in the overarching biblical theme known to Adventists as "the great controversy between Christ and Satan." The rebellion of one of God's most gifted creatures triggered a demonstration of the principles of good and evil and a test of loyalty for each of His free-will beings. This demonstration has been limited by God to a specific period of time. Seventh-day Adventists understand that through the proper application of Bible prophecy, we can know roughly where we stand within the time frame of this conflict. Because of this, we know that we are approaching the very end of this world as we know it. What else do we know?

We know that the devil goes about as a "roaring lion," seeking anyone he can find to devour spiritually (see 1 Peter 5:8). We know that he works individually and corporately to attack God and His people by undermining the message and mission of God's church. We know that his plan is to unite the entire world against God's church—socially, economically, politically, and spiritually. Their worship of him is his ultimate goal.

Many Seventh-day Adventists have noticed the escalated activity in recent years toward globalization in every area of human life. They are also aware that through the accelerated activity of the ecumenical movement, Satan has been drawing together into his global net not only the fragmented elements of Christianity but also of all the religions of the world. He is sparing no person and no church, least of all ours. Why would he give the Adventist church a "pass," allowing us to conduct our business unimpeded? If not alert, we can be pacified into waiting for the familiarity of "end-time troubles," thinking our adversary's interest is more minimal at the present time than it will be later on.

As the controversy continues, he works diligently at every level to bring us all under the influence of his globalist deception. The omega deception is evolving, as we were told it would, for it is "a train of heresies," not just one, and it is on us to test and try the spirits. We have chosen to research a most important end-time strategy: that of the emerging church. While there are other deceptions to choose from, included in this study will be the examination of one of its mechanisms, The One Project, well-embraced in today's Seventh-day Adventist Church. This system, seemingly born out of emerging church theology and culture, appeals to believers to shed their worn-out doctrinal shell of legalistic rituals and come into warm and loving direct contact with Jesus and the vastly more fulfilling, impassioned experience they can find there. The emerging church seeks to tear down denominational barriers—the less doctrine, the more the "church" emerges. My book *The Omega Rebellion* considers Satan's global plan to envelop the Adventist Church along with the rest of the world through Ignatian spirituality and the discipline that carries it: "spiritual formation." Its primary focus is on the preparation of individual believers to be a part of that plan through "spiritual formation" and "contemplative prayer." Some caught up in this movement are now finding rewarding spiritual experiences within The One Project, and we will attempt to explore its genesis and impact.

We are aware that by identifying its forerunners and questioning its methods, we expose ourselves to the accusation of judging; however, "trying the spirits" is scriptural (1 John 4:1). Judging the heart is God's responsibility. He alone can judge unrevealed motives. Yet we are to examine and determine both the teachings and the results of the concepts introduced into the Seventh-day Adventist Church, studying and evaluating their underpinnings and protecting the very lifeblood of our movement.

Perhaps this is the time to clarify the application of the counsel found in Matthew 18. It has been proposed that these instructions must be followed before teachings and thought can be brought to light and appraised. While honest, Spirit-led discussion is surely blessed by God, the counsel to confront one another at a personal level is for sins committed between Christian sisters and brothers, not for the scrutiny of messages publicly and widely dispersed. One would not be expected to reach and discuss the issue with all those who are speaking or writing on the issue; they would simply speak or write as well. The following Ellen White statement makes this clear:

> Her husband seemed to feel unreconciled to my bringing out her faults before the church, and stated that if Sister White had

> followed the counsel in Matthew 18:15–17, he should not have felt hurt. [Matthew 18:15–17 quoted.]
>
> My husband then stated that he should understand that these words of our Lord had reference to cases of personal trespass, and could not be applied in the case of this sister. She had not trespassed against Sister White. But that which had been reproved publicly, was public wrongs which threatened the prosperity of the church and the cause. Here, said my husband, is a text applicable to the case: 1 Timothy 5:20: "Them that sin, rebuke before all, that others may fear." (*Testimonies for the Church*, vol. 2, 15)

If so led, our individual responsibility regarding teachings of concern is to honestly and faithfully hold them up to view; to parse through them for the purpose of understanding. We now believe, along with many others, that emergent church teachings are to be questioned, lest they undermine the mission of the Seventh-day Adventist Church. It is at this level that we focus on this movement in *Meet It*. Does it originate from emergent church leaders who seek globalism and anti-denominationalism, teaching "experiential" religion? Does its theology and culture involve that of those who chose to attend and be instructed by the schools of Babylon? Is this why it has made such headway in our church? If its forerunners have been immersed in the detailed study and training of "emergent" methods from experts in emergent thought and practice, what impact could be expected? Inherent in these questionings is the desire to learn, based on both Scripture and the Spirit of Prophecy, if we err. Consider this:

> There is to be no compromise with those who make void the law of God. It is not safe to rely upon them as counselors. Our testimony is not to be less decided now than formerly; our real position is not to be cloaked in order to please the world's great men. They may desire us to unite with them and accept their plans, and may make propositions in regard to our course of action which may give the enemy an advantage over us. ... Let all your words and works testify, "We have not followed cunningly devised fables" (2 Peter 1:16). "We have also a more sure word of prophecy; whereunto ye do well that ye take heed, as unto a light that shineth in a dark place" (2 Peter 1:19). (*Selected Messages*, book 2, 371)

On the contrary, these are the teachings of which we are to caution the world; we must understand them well enough to provide instruction about and "be ready always to give an answer to every man that asks," thus leading all to the reason of the hope that is in us.

> Let not those who have the truth as it is in Jesus give sanction, even by their silence, to the work of the mystery of iniquity. Let them never cease to sound the note of alarm. Let the education and training of the members of our churches be such that the children and youth among us shall understand there are to be no concessions to this power, the man of sin. Teach them that although the time will come when we can wage the war only at the risk of property and liberty, yet the conflict must be met, in the spirit and meekness of Christ; the truth is to be maintained and advocated as it is in Jesus. Wealth, honor, comfort, home—everything else—is to be a secondary consideration. The truth must not be hid. It must not be denied or disguised, but fully avowed, and boldly proclaimed. (*Selected Messages*, book 2, 369, 370)

The account above can be the beginning of understanding the questioning of the teachings and culture of The One Project and its harmony with emerging church theology as well as the questioning of its harmony with the inspired counsel.

Consider the setting of the final conflict:

> He exerciseth all the power of the first beast before him, and causeth the earth and them which dwell therein to worship the first beast, whose deadly wound was healed. And he doeth great wonders, so that he maketh fire come down from heaven on the earth in the sight of men, and deceiveth them that dwell on the earth by the means of those miracles which he had power to do in the sight of the beast; saying to them that dwell on the earth, that they should make an image to the beast, which had the wound by a sword, and did live. (Revelation 13:12–14)

The ominous and deciding battle of Armageddon looms before us. What clever plans has Satan devised? He has already led the world to an inaccurate translation, deceiving them into believing that the final battle of Armageddon will be a future earthly war waged by the nations of this world in the Middle East's Valley of Megiddo. In examining the word we see that "Armageddon" consists of two words, *har* (*Strong's*, Hebrew word #2022; *Seventh-day Adventist Bible Dictionary*, Armageddon, 71), meaning "mountain," and *meggido*, or *meggidon* (*Strong's* Hebrew word #4023), meaning "place of crowds" or "place of slaughter or cutting, as flesh" in reference to the many battles with Israel's enemies in the ancient Canaanite city of Megiddo. What we have then is God's meaning of "Armageddon": the mountain that rises above the valley of slaughter—Meggido—Mt. Carmel, the "mountain of Megiddo," as Mt. Hood is the mountain of Portland, Oregon, and Mt. Rainier of Seattle, Washington (*Seventh-day Adventist Bible Dictionary*, Meggido, 701) (Also see Louis Were, *The Certainty of the Three Angels Message*, 200; Hans K. LaRondell, ThD, *How to Understand the End-time Prophecies of the Bible* (Bradenton, FL: First Impressions, 1997, 2007).

Mt. Carmel is a mountain with remarkable prophetic significance. It was on its summit that God rained fire from heaven as a witness to those present. He was the true God and His law was the living and active law of the universe. In this conflict, God prevented Satan from raining down fire in answer to the prayers of the prophets of Baal, but it will not be so in the end-time Armageddon. In that battle partially described in Revelation 13:11–18, Satan will be permitted to rain fire down from heaven to deceive all nations into joining with him as he wars against God's people.

The conflict on the summit of Mt. Carmel was over the law of God; the battle of those who rejected it in defiance against the one prophet who stood firm in support of it is a definite picture of the conflict at the end of the world. God's people were deceived by a wicked king and the false prophets of Baal. They needed a supernatural sign from God to make a proper decision, and the Lord in His justice and mercy was there to provide it. Fire rained down from heaven, leading them to acknowledge the one true God.

When the fire at the time of the end rains down from heaven, the three angels' messages will have enlightened every place on earth, and those who refused to accept God's message will stand firm in their arrogance and rejection of God's love and forgiveness, with or without a sign. At this time, Satan is permitted to gather his harvest of lost souls to fill up his forces for the final battle of Armageddon. All nations will fall into the fire's symbolic flames of deception, allying themselves with Satan in his battle against God's people:

> The dragon was wroth with the woman, and went to make war with the remnant of her seed, which keep the commandments of God, and have the testimony of Jesus Christ. (Revelation 12:17)

Without a doubt, there is a war raging. This is not referring to any of the wars that come and go as worldly powers rise and fall, but to the same war that has persisted in our world since Adam and Eve's disobedience in the Garden of Eden, the war between the faithful of God and all the forces of evil in rebellion against Him. This is the universal war between good and evil with the front lines on our planet, the focus of all creation for thousands of years. It is the conflict we opened this chapter with and referred to as the great controversy between Christ and Satan.

This war is not fought with weapons of man's invention; in this war, consequences are decided by acts of the will, by volition. It is a war in which angelic beings contend over the minds of men. Physical and mental battles are fought for us with outcomes predetermined by our choices, for the perfect ways of God demand this dynamic. His love for us reveals itself in our protection when we choose to follow His will. The angelic beings who battle with our enemies in the heavenly spheres advance or retreat in harmony with our choice to love and serve God or not. Our only hope for victory in this war is to abandon self and place ourselves within the tender loving care of our Savior and follow His instructions wherever they may lead.

This war engages every human being, Satan with his angelic army, and every heavenly angel the Lord has assigned to assist us. Jesus is our commander in chief, as is Satan of the forces of evil. No one escapes participation, and we are engaged in battle at every moment in time, whether we know it or not. Whether spiritually lost and pleading for the strength to gain victory, while grappling for resources to survive, or engaged in hypnotic sinful pleasures striving for power, money, or merriment, we are on the front lines of the battlefield. We are forever in combat until life ends, choosing sides by our decisions for good or evil, conscious of what is taking place, or not.

We are at war! Ask the apostles and the countless millions who gave their lives for the Lord, called to follow Jesus in His death on the cross. The light of His selfless love shone brightly through their willingness to die for their Savior. In this war, many victories have been gained by the deaths of God's soldiers, confounding the ranks of the enemy to whom death is defeat, not victory. Determined not to yield the conviction of truth and duty or deny their faith in Jesus, His army of martyrs stood firm unto death.

Ask Peter, hanging upside down on his cross; ask Paul, his head severed from his body by the filthy blade of a gruesome guillotine; ask John the Baptist, whose head was delivered on a platter to a sadistic queen. Ask Stephen, his body crushed and broken under the blast of boulders; ask the apostle John, who just couldn't be killed, even while submerged in boiling oil. Just ask any of them if there is a war going on. Imagine the astonishment and confusion as the apostle John stood before the emperor's throne, the royal carpets being spoiled by dirty oil dripping off his body—oil that was to cook him to oblivion. What was an emperor to do with this disciple who could not be destroyed? It was obvious to all present that this war had supernatural components.

Satan was intent on taking the life of John, who often referred to himself as the disciple whom Jesus continued to love, and who was the last living apostle. When it came to the apostles, Satan was intent on having a perfect record of murder, but it was not to be. The Lord was not going to allow Satan this victory—never. He still had plans for this aged apostle, plans involving you and me, plans essential for finishing His work in this world. John would peer into the realms of glory as no one ever had before. While John was an old man in exile on the Isle of Patmos in the Mediterranean Sea, Jesus appeared to him and opened to his vision heaven itself. This most elaborate vision was to be recorded for all future generations.

The book of Revelation, the final book in the canon of Scripture, not only reveals the world to come but also records the climactic struggle in the universal war between good and evil. Peering through the portals of heaven, it outlines history, exposing Satan and his allies as they attempted to overthrow God's church through the ages. The second half of the book records how God's remnant church, being obedient to its Lord's command and clothed with His righteousness, goes to every nation, kindred, tongue, and people with the gospel message. It records the final, climactic battle in this ongoing war between good and evil, the battle of Armageddon. It records how, after His victory and before the very eyes of His saints, He will create a new world—a world that will be the home of God's faithful and where Jesus will reign as King of kings and Lord of lords forever and ever.

The Lord purposed that the book would enable His army to know its exact position on the battlefield, ever able to hear the instructions of its Commander. The faithful discern the enemy's movements, other than those times when they fall victim to his deceptions and suffer defeat as a part of God's plan for ultimate victory.

You, my friend, are engaged in this war, and as Seventh-day Adventists, you are at the front of the front lines. Here is the problem: Satan has decorated the front lines, creating the illusion that no battle is taking place. He has made the front lines seem like a desirable place to be, hiding all he can that would indicate that a battle is ongoing. The one thing he cannot hide is truth. Those who are unaware of the battle are primarily those who lack knowledge of the truth, of what the issues in the conflict are all about. This is discovered when one searches the inspired words God has given His beloved remnant church, words that warn them of danger. Satan is able to cunningly lead God's people astray because of their failure to "heed the warning God has given" (*Selected Messages*, book 1, 200) that expose his deceptions.

The remnant church has been given the gift of prophecy and the unique understanding of the three angels' messages to proclaim to the world. We have been given inspired instruction on how to fight this war and connect with the divine power needed for victory. Learning to rely on these inspired instructions, and not on the opinions of those who are mystics, spiritualists, and members of the emerging churches of Babylon enables us, advancing us on to victory in Jesus. Because the churches of Babylon have rejected the first and second angels' messages, and have in fact clasped the hand of spiritualism as a unified alliance, they are not being led by God, albeit their people who are seeking truth with honest hearts surely are. But as those organizations have moved through history and continue to move through the roadways of the future, they are facilitating Satan's army, implementing his plans for battle.

The purpose of this book is to consider the battle, what the enemy would have you accept as authentic or legitimate theology, and what he'd have you forfeit in the name of liberty and revival, all the while employing emerging church methods. It will explore the consequence of sitting at the feet of believers of spiritualism as well as the beliefs and impetus behind The One Project, a highly mobile and winsome movement that differs from historic Adventism. It also seeks to do so in a most needful sense of prayerfulness.

The issues regarding the conflict on the top of Mt. Carmel and the end-time Armageddon are alike: the authority and relevance of God's law. This final battle involves the nations attempting to destroy those who have taken a stand for the law of God on earth, as well as God's angels and Satan's fallen angels in the supernatural and spiritual spheres. Every living person is involved in this battle; all are influenced by the supernatural powers in the heavenly realms. With our minds being the "battleground," we are all governed by the good or evil powers in the heavens. The earthly, physical battle rages as the nations attempt to rid the world of God's small group of commandment-keeping followers. The heavenly, supernatural battle is between God's heavenly armies in support of God's people, and Satan's heavenly armies in support of his earthy forces. This is Armageddon.

> For we wrestle not against flesh and blood, but against principalities, against powers, against the rulers of the darkness of this world, against spiritual wickedness in high places. (Ephesians 6:12)

Warfare takes place in high places, or as other translations render it, in heavenly realms or supernatural spheres in the heavens. Without them, without resting in God's hands, we lose. Again, no one escapes this battle—and the battle is now—today. As Inspiration says:

> If our eyes could be open to discern the fallen angels at work with those who feel at ease and consider themselves safe, we would not feel so secure. Evil angels are upon our track every moment. (*Testimonies for the Church*, vol. 1, 302)

> As we walk the streets, or wherever we are, Satan is on our track. (*Sermons and Talks*, vol. 2, 59)

It would follow that there is safety and blessing in following God's plans, not man's. He has given us the gift of prophecy, the unique understanding of the three angels' messages to proclaim to the world and inspired instructions to fight this war, all the while connected with the divine power needed to gain victory. Safety and blessing lies in reliance on the inspired guidance and not on the opinions of the now popular mystics and spiritualists from the churches of Babylon. Finally, coming to terms with the fact that God has not and will not be imparting new light to other churches will gird us to parse through the teachings meant to swerve us off of God's perfect course.

Satan's earthly spiritual vehicle, the Church of Rome and its image, has been and will be the agent through which he facilitates his plan to rule this world. He governs as the Church's rightful ruler, supported unwittingly through its leaders. They administrate but he directs, his right arm of authority influencing this world according to plan. However, many in his church he has not completely won as they have remained unconvinced and stand waiting to understand the danger of entering into the supernatural power offered by the sacramental and mystical worship style. They continue to seek, and desire to know, the truths of God's Word.

Historically, the papacy lost its political power over Europe in 1798, a power it needs as a steppingstone for its worldwide control. The most important part of its plan, its utmost concern: annihilation of that tiny despicable group of Sabbath keepers, whom he loathes.

In this planet's closing events, Satan's cleverness and craft will be hidden from the casual observer. Knowing God and His character and remaining closely connected as He intercedes for them will bring His people home without harm.

Paralleling his work to destroy this group of God's true believers, it is his strategy to unite all of Christianity's fragmented groups, through his new deceptive movement called the emerging church. Doctrines and cultures, the two most powerful characteristics that keep denominations distinct and separate, are made of none effect. Denounced as old-world trappings, they are replaced by revival and experiential religion. Thus, it remains the task of God's church to determine whether these things are false or authentic. Following the theological trail, understanding its genesis and intent would have to be a part of the determination.

While caring and thoughtful Seventh-day Adventists teach and present these emerging church concepts, and the number of believers experiencing what they perceive to be true spirituality swells, their counterparts or they themselves have been taught at the feet of self-proclaimed mystics and spiritualists. Why? Why mix the Word of God with the word of Satan? Does it not behoove the presenters to question the mixture and the origin?

Yet it has been presented as reinventing the Adventist wheel, the better way, Adventism at its best. The barrier of yesterday, the "dead" style of Christianity is altogether gone and replaced by something better. Unnoticed though, are the distinctive doctrines that are also gone, like the law of God. Since God's law is a revelation of His character, who is the Jesus being worshipped? While the all-absorbing experience is ultimately appreciated, the adversary quietly steals his way into God's true church; he then destroys confidence in such God-given protections as the Spirit of Prophecy, whereas without trusting in and heeding its warnings, we will surely be led astray.

This is not the first time this has occurred among God's remnant church. More than 100 years ago we found ourselves in the midst of a crisis so serious that the Lord Himself had to take immediate control of the ship (church) to keep it from sinking as it struck the iceberg of the "alpha."

Chapter Two:
The Alpha and the Omega

In this chapter, we will do our best to understand what Ellen White intended when she used the words "alpha," and/or "omega," words she intended to identify the most dangerous deceptions that would ever confront the Seventh-day Adventist Church.

> As we read, I recognized the very sentiments against which I had been bidden to speak in warning during the early days of my public labors. When I first left the State of Maine, it was to go through Vermont and Massachusetts, to bear a testimony against these sentiments. *The Living Temple* contains the *alpha* of these theories. I knew that the *omega* would follow in a little while; and I *trembled* for our people. (*Selected Messages,* book 1, 203, emphasis added)

We will attempt to understand just what Ellen White may have meant when she said, "Those who entertain these sophistries will soon find themselves in a position where the enemy can talk with them" (*The Review and Herald*, October 22, 1903). This frightening concept may be applicable to experiences some are having in our ranks currently, matters that are "omega-like" to God's people.

It is important to understand that it was not only Dr. Kellogg's *theology* that needed to be addressed but also his use of *psychological techniques of mind control* while he was at the helm of the largest and most influential institution of the church and one of the largest in the world. This placed the doctor and the leaders under Satan's influence, in the bull's eye of his attacks against the church.

Satan had already led the doctor astray, so the leaders of the church were precisely where Satan wanted them to be to carry out his destructive work. When leaders can be deceived, they are of the greatest use to the arch deceiver. The deception of the leaders in Kellogg's day, identified as the "alpha," contains many similarities as to how the future "omega" deception will operate. This final satanic evil will appear as yet another in a "train of heresies" as the close of probation approaches.

Under the Lord's direction, Ellen White sent a number of warnings to convey how these dangerous theories were leading our medical workers astray. A sixty-page pamphlet, *Testimonies for the Church Containing Letters to Physicians and Ministers Instruction to Seventh-day Adventists* (1904), was published.

For upwards of twenty years, Ellen White agonized in prayer for the wayward doctor, for whom she had great love and concern. It was her mentoring and assistance that enabled him to receive the education needed to fill the position to which the Lord had called him. In a letter she wrote to him in November of 1902, she said:

> I love your soul and I want you to have eternal life. I must tell you the truth. And whether you acknowledge it or not, you know that what I tell you is truth.
>
> Shortly before your father died, he called me to him, saying that he had something to say to me. "I feel that John is in great danger," he said. "But, Sister White, you will not get discouraged, will you, even though he seems to be headstrong? You are the only one who can help him. Do not let him go, even though his case appears discouraging."
>
> I promised that I would do as the Spirit of the Lord directed me. God's word to me has always been, "You can help him." (*Manuscript Releases,* vol. 12, 3, 4)

The emotional pain Ellen White endured as she watched this brilliant and dedicated son, friend, and physician slip beyond the reach of the Holy Spirit's influence must have been heart-wrenching. Consider her feelings while writing these final words of warning to Dr. Kellogg after his continued refusal to heed her inspired counsels:

> I have the tenderest feelings toward Dr. Kellogg. For many years I have tried to hold fast to him. God's word to me has always been, "You can help him." Sometimes I am awakened in the night, and,

> rising, I walk the room, praying: "O Lord, hold Dr. Kellogg fast. Do not let him go. Keep him steadfast. Anoint his eyes with the heavenly eye salve, that he may see all things clearly." Night after night I have lain awake, studying how I could help him. Earnestly and often I have prayed that the Lord may not permit him to turn away from sanctifying truth. This is the burden that weighs me down,—the desire that he shall be kept from making mistakes that would hurt his soul and injure the cause of present truth. But for some time his actions have revealed that a strange spirit is controlling him. The Lord will take this matter in His own hands. I must bear the messages of warning that God gives me to bear, and then leave with the Lord the results. I must now present the matter in all its bearings; for the people of God must not be despoiled." (*Testimonies for the Church Containing Letters to Physicians and Ministers Instruction to Seventh-day Adventists*, 58, 59)

Ellen White loved Dr. Kellogg's soul. The way she hung on to the hope and studied how she might help him gives us insight into the heart of love and concern that the Lord's messenger had for one who was falling away from the truth. It reveals how God filled her heart with the same tender care and forgiveness that Jesus has for each and every one of us. It is an encouragement to realize that the Lord chose a person truly converted and sanctified by the Spirit of God to watch over His children and give them divine counsel.

The way she loved and counseled Dr. Kellogg is an example for us of how to love and care for the misdirected in our churches and families. She labored year after year, writing letter after letter, entreating the doctor to turn from the theories that beclouded his mind. She meticulously pointed out every aspect of his mistaken theology and leadership style, promising him the Lord's love and acceptance if he would only surrender, but he would not.

Longsuffering reached its limit. With a tear, the waiting time had to end, and action was necessary to save God's church. She said, "The people of God must not be despoiled;" the gift of salvation must not be stolen from God's children by these false and deceptive theories. The patient waiting for Dr. Kellogg to respond to the pleadings of the Holy Spirit had to come to an end. God's people must be saved. As the Lord's messenger, Ellen White was forever vigilant in her watch care over the people of God. The Lord revealed to her the changes that would have taken place in the structure of the church if Dr. Kellogg and his associates had implemented their plans.

> The enemy of souls has sought to bring in the supposition that a great reformation was to take place among Seventh-day Adventists, and that this reformation would consist in giving up the doctrines which stand as the pillars of our faith, and engaging in a process of reorganization. Were this reformation to take place, what would result? The principles of truth that God in His wisdom has given to the remnant church would be discarded. Our religion would be changed. The fundamental principles that have sustained the work for the last fifty years would be accounted as error. A new organization would be established. Books of a new order would be written. A system of intellectual philosophy would be introduced. The founders of this system would go into the cities, and do a wonderful work. The Sabbath, of course, would be lightly regarded, as also the God who created it. Nothing would be allowed to stand in the way of the new movement. The leaders would teach that virtue is better than vice, but God being removed, they would place their dependence on human power, which, without God, is worthless. Their foundation would be built on the sand, and storm and tempest would sweep away the structure.
>
> Who has authority to begin such a movement? We have our Bibles. We have our experience, attested to by the miraculous working of the Holy Spirit. We have a truth that admits of no compromise. Shall we not repudiate everything that is not in harmony with this truth? (*Selected Messages,* book 1, 204, 205)

Here we have an inspired statement of the changes that would have taken place in the church if the "alpha" of apostasy had been successful. Dr. Kellogg's apostasy included controlling minds, the resistance of inspired counsel, self-exaltation, the misuse of church funds, and his insistence in advocating false theories concerning the personality and presence of God. This was, however, just the beginning. She termed this beginning phase the "alpha," implying that forms of this deception will arise again and again, reaching its final mature stage just before the end of time. Many have envisioned the "omega" as something separate and distinct from the "alpha," but that theory does not correspond with the way Ellen White used the terms "alpha" and "omega." These words were a regular part of her vocabulary and she used them together or separately, in reference to the beginning or the ending, or to the entire cycle of beginning to ending, for many subjects. Let's look at a few examples.

> [Read] a Book containing the words of Him who is the Alpha and Omega of wisdom. The time spent in a study of these books might better be spent in gaining a knowledge of Him whom to know aright is life eternal. (*Counsels on Health,* 369)

Here she refers to Jesus as the "Alpha and Omega of wisdom."

> I think we should consider that problem. If there are those who do not want to send their children to our school, at which preparation is given for the future eternal life, to learn here the Alpha of how they should conduct themselves for the Omega, the end, then they can take their children and put them where they please. (*Manuscript Releases,* vol. 6, 373)

Here, alpha is in reference to the beginning of education, learning how to conduct themselves in preparation for "the Omega, the end," the end of all things.

> Here we have the Alpha of Genesis and the Omega of Revelation. The blessing is promised to all those who keep the commandments of God, and who co-operate with him in the proclamation of the third angel's message. (*The Review and Herald,* June 8, 1897)

This is a reference to the beginning and end of Scripture.

> "I thank the Lord that the work is begun in Washington. I am glad that the publishing work has been moved from Battle Creek to Washington, and that plans are being laid for the establishment of a sanitarium in Washington. We see the Alpha, and we know that Christ is also the Omega." (*The $150,000 Fund,* Pamphlet 143, 8).

The alpha here is the beginning of the publishing work in Washington. It will succeed because Christ is also the "Omega," and will be with the work until the end.

> In all that we do or say, in all our expenditure of means, we are to strive with full purpose of heart to fulfill the purpose of him who is the Alpha and Omega of medical missionary work. Beside all waters we are to sow the seeds of truth, winning souls to Christ by tender compassion and unselfish interest. (*The Review and Herald*, May 5, 1904)

Here we learn that Jesus is the "Alpha and Omega of medical missionary work." These are a few examples of her use of alpha and omega, demonstrating her frequent use of these terms. How did she apply them to the dangerous theories of Dr. Kellogg? A few references follow.

> The work of advancement in the proclamation of truth has at such times been greatly hindered [by] specious workings, which are the *Alpha of the Omega*, which means very much to the people who are in any way connected with parties who have received the warnings of the Lord, but refused to heed them. (*Manuscript Releases*, vol. 11, 211, emphasis added)

Notice "specious workings, which are the Alpha of the Omega." Here and in other places, she refers to the "alpha" as being part of the "omega." Examine the following:

> One, and another, and still another are presented to me as having been led to accept the pleasing fables that mean the sanctification of sin. *Living Temple* contains the *alpha of a train of heresies*. …
>
> I was instructed that the ideas they had accepted were but the *alpha of a great deception*. I had to meet similar delusions in Portsmouth and in Boston. (*Manuscript Releases*, vol. 11, 247, emphasis added)

The alpha was simply the first of a great deception.

> During the General Conference of 1901 the Lord warned me against sentiments that were then held by Brethren Prescott and Waggoner. These sentiments have been as leaven put into meal. Many minds have received them. The ideas of some regarding a great experience supposed to be sanctification have been *the*

alpha of a train of deception. (*Manuscript Releases*, vol. 10, 87, emphasis added)

Sometimes "alpha" is used concerning false theories that mean "the sanctification of sin" (*Manuscript Releases*, vol. 11, 247), as in the book *The Living Temple*. Other times it refers to deceptions during the early stages of the work in Portsmouth and Boston. Prescott and Waggoner shared sentiments concerning sanctification that she labeled the *"alpha of a train of deception."*

Considering the many usages of "alpha" and "omega" in the context of the end-time threat to the Seventh-day Adventist Church, what emerges is this: Satan is at war with the remnant church and does not cease his deceptive activity. When he is exposed in one deception, he manufactures another. This compilation of satanic devices against the remnant church, over its entire existence during the "time of the end," is the "omega." This "train of heresies" has a beginning and will have an end. The deceptions in the beginning of our work in Boston and Portsmouth, leading up to and primarily surrounding Dr. Kellogg's apostasy, especially the pantheism in *The Living Temple*, Ellen White termed "the Alpha of the Omega" (*Manuscript Releases*, vol. 11, 211), and sometimes just "the alpha." She implied that this future final deception against the church will be the omega of the omega or simply "the omega."

The following is a summary of facts about the "alpha" and what would have happened had the church not heeded the warning. It is mostly compiled from two chapters on the alpha and omega found in *Selected Messages*, book 1.

The Alpha

- It "would lead astray the minds of those who are not thoroughly established in the foundational principles of present truth" (page 202).
- It would "undermine the foundations of our faith" (page 196).
- It consists of the teachings and "doctrines of devils" (page 197).
- "The Scripture [when] used to substantiate the doctrine … set forth is Scripture misapplied" (page 203).

- "The spiritualistic theories regarding the personality of God, followed to their logical conclusion, [would] sweep away the whole Christian economy" (page 203).
- "They make of no effect the truth of heavenly origin, and rob the people of God of their past experience, giving them instead a false science" (page 203).
- "The principles of truth that God in His wisdom has given to the remnant church, would be discarded" (page 204).
- "Our religion would be changed. The fundamental principles that have sustained the work for the last fifty years would be accounted as error" (page 204).
- "Books of a new order would be written" (page 204).
- "Nothing would be allowed to stand in the way of the new movement" (page 205).
- It would delude those not willing to heed the warning (page 200).
- "The omega will follow, and will be received by those who are not willing to heed the warning God has given" (page 200).
- The people who were deceived and who would have brought on the alpha in a form of Satan's "hypnotism." (*Manuscript Releases*, vol. 10, 163)

Remember, the "alpha" was the "Alpha *of* the Omega," the beginning deception in that train of heresies, with the ultimate end-time deception arriving just before probation closes. Many, if not all, of the characteristics of the alpha may be included in the omega, but we can be assured that the omega will be beyond anything we have imagined up to this point. Why is this? It is because it made Ellen White tremble for the safety of the church, and she was startled when she beheld it (see *Selected Messages*, book 1, 203).

So what can we expect from the "omega"? Here is a summary from *Selected Messages*, book 1. Notice how the removal of the pillars of our faith is one of the dangers of the omega and how its acceptance would sweep away the entire Christian economy.

The Omega

- It will "rob the people of God of their past experience, giving them instead a false science" (page 204).
- Receiving these theories will "undermine the foundation pillars of our faith," especially Christ's ministry in the most holy place and the three angels' messages (page 196).
- "Those who entertain these sophistries will soon find themselves in a position where [Satan] can talk with them, and lead them away from God" (page 202).
- The omega introduces that which is naught but speculation in regard to "the presence and personality of God" (page 202).
- "The omega will be of a most startling nature." (*Selected Messages,* Book 1, 197)
- It will result in the "control of human minds." (*Manuscript Releases,* vol. 13, 394)

The spiritual revival that grew into the Seventh-day Adventist Church is identified in Revelation, chapter 10, and immediately followed the event characterized by the blowing of the sixth trumpet in August of 1840. That spiritual revival was forecast to arise at the end of the longest time prophecy in the Bible, the 2,300 days of Daniel 8:14. It is also known in history to this day as the Great Awakening, the greatest Christian revival since apostolic times. We will study the history of this amazing experience out of which came the remnant church of Revelation 12:17: "The dragon was wroth with the woman, and went to make war with the *remnant of her seed,* which keep the commandments of God, and have the testimony of Jesus Christ" (emphasis supplied). Their experience was unique and most trying.[2]

After the Great Disappointment in the autumn of 1844, only a few faithful Adventists emerged, a small fellowship of believers who refused to give in to the temptation to abandon ship. They knew it was their Lord and Savior who led them through this most trying experience. They had a close and definite relationship with Him, knowing His voice personally.

2 For more information on this topic, please see Rick Howard's book entitled *The Omega Rebellion*, chapter 5, "Who Are We Anyway? Part II." Coldwater, MI: Remnant Publications, 2012.

They had no doubt that they were following their Lord as He directed, even though the outcome was not what they expected.

As they persisted to search out the meaning of their experience, pleading with God for better understanding, He opened their minds to the most profound and thorough understanding of Scripture. As this small, dedicated group of faithful Bible students continued searching, Christ's ministry in the heavenly sanctuary was opened to their understanding, explaining the reason for the Great Disappointment. Shortly thereafter, the truth of the Sabbath was presented to them. As they studied under the guidance of the Holy Spirit, they saw how the seventh-day Sabbath had been neglected for almost 2,000 years, and they then determined to begin to live according to this newly discovered Bible truth. The Spirit of Prophecy was then revived in the church and verified the new truths that were constantly being revealed as they all continued to study together.

As they searched the Scriptures with the diligence of the Bereans, the Lord unfolded to their eager minds the change in Christ's ministry that took place on October 22, 1844. Jesus began the final phase of the work of the atonement, entering into the most holy place of the heavenly sanctuary on that day, providing "a new and living way which He has consecrated for us, through the veil" where we are to have "boldness to enter into the Holiest by the blood of Jesus" (Hebrews 10:20, 19).

It is our discovery and acceptance of two wonderful truths—that it is the love of Christ that drives us to "keep the commandments of God" (Revelation 14:12), and that we have in our midst the Spirit of Prophecy (Revelation 19:10) that verifies that we are God's remnant church. It was and is the absolute rejection of these very truths by every other Protestant and Christian denomination that makes them the daughters or harlots of Babylon (see Revelation 17:5).

According to the Spirit of Prophecy, the "omega" will lead to the denial of these precious truths, the very beliefs that make us God's chosen people.

Chapter Three:
Warnings

It's not easy these days for Adventists to choose reading material, especially the kind that will actually improve their spiritual lives. We are inundated with Christian books, CDs, and DVDs that promise all kinds of blessings. What can we believe? How can we be sure? We decided to include this section in order to study the subject of reading non-SDA material and pray that it will be helpful.

Consider this: the Lord longs for us to know how much He loves us. So any new "spiritual" light or teaching that will benefit our personal or spiritual lives, or the work and mission of God's church, He will give to us without our having to be exposed to the risks involved in attempting to separate these kinds of truths from the errors existing in the voluminous materials of fallen Babylon. We are His denominated and greatly beloved bride, whom He protects at all cost and would never think of sending back to the fallen churches of Babylon to discover new and helpful spiritual teachings. These are the very same churches He delivered us from. It would be like sending Daniel back into the lion's den after saving him from it. Those in God's church today, like Daniel, have been delivered. Let's simply rejoice in our deliverance and be free in the Lord, free from the errors that abound in the fallen churches.

In spite of these wonderful truths, many Adventists believe they can wade through the mixture of truth and error found in all the writings of fragmented Christianity, choosing only the good while discarding the bad. We have been practicing this method for decades. Just think of all the books, seminars, videos, and CDs that have influenced Adventists over the years; examples like the books by Rick Warren, John Hagee, Steve Chapman, Tony Campolo, and on and on abound. As the Lord led me from church district to church district, well-meaning church members would give me books by these and other authors. For instance, I have multiple copies of Rick Warren's *The Purpose Driven Life* in my library (skimmed, but mostly unread). Fellow Adventists: in the light of His own instruction, wading through this mixture of truth and error to find tidbits of "new light" could not be a strategy the Lord would sanction, for Inspiration counsels us:

> If God has any new light to communicate, He will let His chosen and beloved understand it, without their going to have *their minds enlightened by hearing those who are in darkness and error. (Early Writings*, 124, emphasis added)

This statement is simple and straightforward, and one from which we can conclude that God will not send us to meetings or have us examine teachings that are a mixture of truth and error in order to find new light. This would include books and other documents written by those in the churches we consider "fallen," churches that rejected the advancing truths of the Reformation, the first and second angels' messages given in the summer of 1844.

The warning in the statement above is only in reference to light meant to improve our spiritual lives or that adds to the mission of our church and is not referring to analyzing these writings or doing research for educational purposes. To believe God is leading us to discover hidden light necessitates the violation of God's counsel, for it says in the inspired statement above that He will always shine new "light" on us without our having to go to "those who are in darkness and error." One of the reasons God raised up His remnant church after the Great Awakening was to correct the abundant error that existed in the Protestant world up to that time. The Lord, in calling together His chosen end-time church, wanted His people to have a pure and accurate understanding of doctrine and mission. This doctrine would separate them from the fallen churches as He led them into an understanding of Christ's ministry in the heavenly temple and the unique mission of giving the three angels' messages to the world. They were to be His spiritual Israel, unique and separated from the influences of modern Babylon.

Some disagree with this interpretation of the Spirit of Prophecy and often cite the fact that even Ellen White's personal library contained books written by members of the very churches we say to avoid when searching for "light." There are some important spiritual consequences that need to be considered by those who believe this way.

First is that most of the books referred to by Ellen White, from which she quoted in her writings, were in fact written by members of God's true church, the Protestant churches of the day; they were from God's church because this was before they denominationally rejected the first and second angel's messages. She speaks of and quotes the reformers from William Miller backwards mentioning names like Wesley, Bunyan, and Baxter, etc.—all who wrote well before 1844. They were all members of God's true church at the time they wrote and preached. To claim that because they were Presbyterian or Baptist at the time they wrote, we can read and search for light from today's authors in those now fallen denominations, is faulty reasoning and violates Ellen White's own counsel in the Spirit of Prophecy. It should be noted that these churches did not all fall at once, and all together made up God's true church until they were officially pronounced fallen by Inspiration, sometime after 1844.

Second, and most important, we are not prophets and do not have the special gifts the Lord gave His messenger. It is true that Ellen White read and quoted from some from material written after the denominational churches were pronounced fallen, such as *The Life and Epistles of St. Paul* by W. J. Conybeare and J.S. Howson, which was published in 1856, and Edersheim's work *The Life and Times of Jesus the Messiah*, which was published in 1883. While the aforementioned books that Ellen White read and used in preparing *The Desire of Ages* and *Acts of the Apostles* are all from non-Adventist authors, we must remember that she was given special discernment concerning what to choose that agreed with what she wanted to write; in this task, she was divinely led to only that which is truth. For us to believe that we would be led this way is wrong and presumptuous thinking. When Ellen White recommended Conybeare and Howson's book, she specifically noted its usefulness to the earnest student of the New Testament and did not point to its spiritual usefulness in the personal Christian walk. We read, "The Life of St. Paul by Conybeare and Howson, I regard as a book of great merit, and one of rare usefulness to the earnest student of the New Testament history."[3]

Here is an explanation of the special gifts God blesses His prophets with from *Ellen White and Her Critics*: "The uniqueness of the prophet is that in a wholly distinctive manner his mind is illumined by God to write only truth. If he finds that a Bible commentator has aptly and tersely stated a truth why should the borrowing of that terse statement prove that the

3 Arthur L. White, *Ellen G. White: Volume 3—The Lonely Years: 1876–1891*, 215.

prophet is a fraud? We think it may reasonably prove the opposite. Only a prophet of God could know with certainty whether a particular statement by some writer presented a great truth in wholly accurate form." (EGW and Her Critics, p. 461)

To attempt to justify our use of writings from the fallen churches in search of spiritual light or ideas that alter the mission of God's church on the premise that God's messenger used these writings is to put forward an argument that cannot stand in the light of all the counsel we have from her own pen. With this understood, it is true that as time continues, knowledge will increase. There has been and will be new "light" in many areas other than those spiritual subjects that were rejected by the fallen churches. New discoveries in the field of health are at the top of the list. No doubt this is why we are counseled in the Spirit of Prophecy to search and read the best authors in the areas of research that affect Christian life. On the one hand, we read:

> Our workers should use their knowledge of the laws of life and health. They should study from cause to effect. Read the best authors on these subjects, and obey religiously that which your reason tells you is truth. (*Counsels on Health*, 566)

On the other hand, we find this:

> God is displeased with us when we go to listen to error, without being obliged to go. (*Early Writings*, 125)

> Just as long as men consent to listen to these sophistries, a subtle influence will weave the fine threads of these seductive theories into their minds, and men who should turn away from the first sound of such teaching will learn to love it, (*Manuscript Releases*, vol. 10, 163)

It seems that the study of books about life and health lies within the scope of subjects we are instructed to search from "the best authors," subjects where the Lord will lead us individually to find new light. How do we explain all of this?

These are subjects that were not included in what the fallen churches rejected and are important for us to research, for as time goes on we will constantly make discoveries that will improve our health. All new discoveries still need to be weighed against the light we already have in the Spirit of Prophecy.

With this in mind, we are also counseled not to listen to mixtures of truth and error coming from those churches that rejected the first and second angels' messages when they were given. Our basic doctrines and understanding of Scripture—the sanctuary, state of the dead, and second coming, among others—are not going to change. The fallen churches cannot offer us any light on these subjects, only darkness (see Isaiah 8:20).

The early Adventists painstakingly discovered the truth explaining the Great Disappointment and the change in Christ's ministry in heaven. They shared these truths with the world's Christian denominations and those denominations rejected them. The fallen churches had their opportunity to accept truth but did not. It is for this reason that we are warned not to go to them for light—they have none. This does not negate the fact that they are filled with God's children, who are following the light they have. Their salvation and our call for them come out—"Come out of her my people" (Revelation 18:1-4)—is our mission. Please consider what you are about to read concerning these churches carefully. The Spirit of Prophecy says that Satan stands at the helm of these churches.

> Satan has a large confederacy, his church. Christ calls it the synagogue of Satan because the members are the children of sin. The members of Satan's church have been constantly working to cast off the divine law, and confuse the distinction between good and evil. Satan is working with great power in and through the children of disobedience to exalt treason and apostasy as truth and loyalty. And at this time the power of his satanic inspiration is moving the living agencies to carry out the great rebellion against God that commenced in heaven. (*Testimonies for Ministers and Gospel Workers*, 16)

The danger for us is in believing that these churches have new light to offer and not discerning that it is not light but darkness.

> Said the angel, Nothing less than the whole armor of righteousness can overcome, and retain the victory over the powers of darkness. Satan has taken full possession of the churches as a body. The sayings and doings of men are dwelt upon instead of the plain cutting truths of the word of God....

> I saw that since Jesus had left the Holy place of the heavenly Sanctuary, and had entered within the second veil, the churches were left as were the Jews; and they have been filling up with every unclean and hateful bird. I saw great iniquity and vileness in the churches; yet they profess to be Christians. (See *Early Writings*, 273–275)

God also has a church:

> "For I know that the Lord is great, and that our Lord is above all gods." Consider, my brethren and sisters, that the Lord has a people, a chosen people, His church, to be His own, His own fortress, which He holds in a sin-stricken, revolted world; and *He intended that no authority should be known in it, no laws be acknowledged by it, but His own.* (*Testimonies for Ministers and Gospel Workers*, 15, emphasis added)

> Christ has said of His people, "Ye are the light of the world." *We are the Lord's denominated people*, to proclaim the truths of heavenly origin. The most solemn, sacred work ever given to mortals is the proclamation of the first, second, and third angels' messages to our world. (*Counsels on Diet and Foods*, 76, emphasis added)

The meaning of all this is not hard to understand. In the materials prepared by those in the "fallen" churches, we are counseled not to search for "light" that may be applicable to our spiritual lives or to the mission and work of our church. It is there, but inspired counsel reveals that it is a trap laid by the enemy to have us believe it is possible to discern between truth and the error that is also there without making dangerous mistakes—mistakes that will eventually lead us astray. This is why the Lord says not to search this material for instruction on spiritual growth. God is God and He has reasons for this counsel. Satan has set a snare, baiting with that which is very enticing to the fallen nature. Something we are always hungry for is acceptance by our colleagues, both professionally and intellectually. After all, who wants to be viewed as insecure isolationists, especially by a Christian world that considers itself in the midst of a revival and a period of tremendous spiritual growth? We should seriously consider if we are trying to keep up with and be respected by this deceived Christian community, and if we are rejecting the inspired truth that claims that they are the fallen Babylon we are to be warning the world about.

Once again, to clarify, we are warned against seeking for light in areas of spiritual growth and the mission and work of the church, among the teachings in the fallen churches of Babylon. Concerning these subjects, the Lord has said that if He has light for us, He will give it to us without our having to return to those churches that are fallen and in darkness and error.

> If God has delivered us from such darkness and error, we should stand fast in the liberty wherewith He has set us free and rejoice in the truth. God is displeased with us when we go to listen to error, without being obliged to go, for unless He sends us to those meetings where error is forced home to the people by the power of the will, He will not keep us. (*Early Writings*, 124, 125)

What is the meaning of this statement? The admonition not to go to their meetings means that God does not want their words to influence our thinking—so don't listen or watch. For the twenty-first century, we can apply this counsel to mean not only should we avoid going to their meetings, we also shouldn't listen to their CDs, MP3s, online presentations (including YouTube), or watch their DVDs. God loves us and desires us to "be separate from those…imbibing new errors," and God's counsel is "that neither young nor old should attend their meetings" (*Early Writings*, 124). "Their meetings" applies to those sponsored by the churches we know teach a mixture of truth and error, which Ellen White called the "fallen churches."

> The fallen denominational churches are Babylon. (*Evangelism*, 365)

These are meetings held by other denominational groups of Christians outside of the Seventh-day Adventist Church, His only true denominated people. All other Protestant denominations are identified as "fallen" in the Spirit of Prophecy, having rejected the first and second angels' messages when they were first given. This is no different than the counsel God gave the Israelites concerning mingling (see the section in the Introduction entitled "Solomon's Fall—Why?") with the heathen nations surrounding them. The principle is the same, and His counsel to us is the same because we are today's Israel. God has not changed.

We need to be careful not to fall into the emotional trap of accepting the teachings of the fallen churches because we love their members and yearn for their deliverance. The second angel's message calls them out of those churches and does not call for us to join them. We may not be spiritually prepared at present to receive them, needing revival ourselves, but this does not mean that the Lord desires for us to attempt to separate out truth from the mixture of truth and error that they teach; neither does it mean we should join them in their false and dangerous worship services and revivals.

There is also a temptation for us to be challenged to reach up to the supposed higher educational standards the world has imposed on schools of higher learning in the belief that we must also meet these worldly standards to remain credible. If we follow God's instruction, we will never be considered credible by the world. The pressure to keep up with the world in our institutions can be overwhelming, but if allowed to control us, the world will contaminate our understanding of "the most solemn, sacred work ever given to mortals"—the three angels' messages (*Counsels on Diet and Foods*, 76).

Chapter Four:
Globalism

As we begin to address the issues in the church that we love and believe has been called to proclaim a special message to the world, there are two words of interest: "globalism" and "globalization."

Globalism can mean different things, such as policies that place the interests of the entire world above those of individual nations, or the consideration of the entire world as a proper sphere for one nation to project political influence, therefore control, over the whole world.

From the Internet's Wikipedia, here is the definition for globalization:

> The term globalization ... refers to processes of international integration arising from the interchange of world views, products, ideas, and other aspects of culture. Advances in transportation and telecommunications infrastructure, including the rise of the Internet, are major factors in globalization, generating further interdependence of economic and cultural activities.[4]

> Globalization describes the interplay across cultures of macro-social forces. These forces include religion, politics, and economics. Globalization can erode and universalize the characteristics of a local group.[5]

Seventh-day Adventists generally believe the world's future includes the globalization of the world both politically and spiritually. It is not

---

4 Globalization, Wikipedia: The Free Encyclopedia, http://en.wikipedia.org/wiki/Globalization, (accessed February 12, 2014).

5 Sara Rodriguez Cubillas, "The effects of ERP's in the globalization strategy of corporations," Prezi, http://prezi.com/so0rmisrpz6k/the-effects-of-erps-in-the-globalization-strategy-of-corporations/ (accessed February 12, 2014).

something we strive for, but it is something we acknowledge is going to happen. Although it has become unpopular over the last fifty years for Adventists to proclaim a belief in globalization, it is nonetheless a fact of our prophetic identity since we believe it will take place. The Spirit of Prophecy supports this:

> The Protestant churches are in great darkness, or they would discern the signs of the times. The Roman Church is far-reaching in her plans and modes of operation. She is employing every device to extend her influence and increase her power in preparation for a fierce and determined conflict to regain control of the world, to re-establish persecution, and to undo all that Protestantism has done. Catholicism is gaining ground upon every side. …
>
> The influence of Rome in the countries that once acknowledged her dominion is still far from being destroyed. And prophecy foretells a restoration of her power. "I saw one of his heads as it were wounded to death; and his deadly wound was healed: and all the world wondered after the beast." Rev. 13:3. The infliction of the deadly wound points to the abolition of the papacy in 1798. After this, says the prophet, "His deadly wound was healed; and all the world wondered after the beast." Paul states plainly that the man of sin will continue until the second advent. 2 Thess. 2:8. To the very close of time he will carry forward his work of deception. And the Revelator declares, also referring to the papacy, "All that dwell upon the earth shall worship him, whose names are not written in the book of life." Revelation 13:8
>
> Protestants little know what they are doing when they propose to accept the aid of Rome in the work of Sunday exaltation. While they are bent upon the accomplishment of their purpose, Rome is aiming to re-establish her power, to recover her lost supremacy. Let history testify of her artful and persistent efforts to insinuate herself into the affairs of nations; and having gained a foothold, to further her own aims, even at the ruin of princes and people. Romanism openly puts forth the claim that the pope "can pronounce sentences and judgments in contradiction to the *right of nations, to the law of God and man.*"

> God's Word has given warning of the impending danger; let this be unheeded, and the Protestant world will learn what the purposes of Rome really are, only when it is too late to escape the snare. She is silently growing into power. Her doctrines are exerting their influence in legislative halls, in the churches, and in the hearts of men. She is piling up her lofty and massive structures, in the secret recesses of which her former persecutions will be repeated. Stealthily and unsuspectedly she is strengthening her forces to further her own ends when the time shall come for her to strike. All that she desires is vantage-ground, and this is already being given her. We shall soon see and shall feel what the purpose of the Roman element is. Whoever shall believe and obey the Word of God will thereby incur reproach and persecution. (*The Great Controversy*, 1888 ed., 565, 579–581)

These encouraging statements given to the messenger of the Lord are meant to inspire, to protect, and to warn us of the very things happening in the world now—right now! Please consider these words carefully and prayerfully. To summarize: the context of these statements is clear—the political/religious empire of Rome is about to regain control of the world for the final conflict outlined in the Spirit of Prophecy and in Scripture. To paraphrase Ellen White's statements: Rome is aiming to reestablish and restore her power by insinuating herself into the affairs of nations to further her own ends, which are to control the world, to bring back persecution, and to undo all that Protestantism has done until the entire world "wonders" after the beast. That is what the Spirit of Prophecy claims the future holds.

Many in the church today have trouble accepting what has been foretold in the Spirit of Prophecy. They feel it is arrogant to think of ourselves as God's chosen people or to believe that we have present truth, etc. Many feel the Roman Catholic Church has changed her ways and is not the same as she was when Ellen White was alive.

Roman Catholicism has not changed, and the only way to continue to believe that she has changed is to reject the inspiration of Scripture ("all the world wondered after the beast") and the Spirit of Prophecy. If Rome had changed, there would be no truth in *The Great Controversy* and no need to spread the three angels' messages—just what Satan desires. The well-known Adventist theologian Dr. Alberto Treiyer puts it this way:

> The Vatican is continuously calling the nations of the earth to unite in a "globalization of solidarity," which means to resign regional, racial, nationalistic, and religious segregation. In the confrontation of civilizations it is necessary, says the pope, to open dialogue and interrelate to each other. Like the builders of Babel at the beginning of human history, he is pushing the United Nations to have "one language," that is, to agree upon global common concepts and share "a common speech" (Genesis 11:1, 7). He wants a world united under "one [ruling] city" (Rev. 17:5, 18), with "one tower" to occupy the place of God (see Isa. 14:12–14), to be "one people" with "one name" (Gen. 11:4, 6) … "the name of the beast or the number of his name" … (Rev. 13:17). [6]

The question is: why do so many in our church believe this deception today? It seems that the desire to be "friends" with the fallen churches and to be accepted into the sisterhood of all Christians is frustrating because Adventists are considered "odd" or "peculiar" by those of other faiths. The fact that we are nearly the only Protestant denomination that continues to "protest" against the errors of Roman Catholicism, expose those errors in preparation for the Lord's return, and identify Rome openly as the antichrist and the beast of Revelation 13, stands in the way of our being accepted by other Christians, an acceptance many Adventists greatly desire.

Much of this problem stems from Adventists' lack of understanding of what the Seventh-day Adventist Church is, how God specifically called us as His remnant people, and that the message He has given us for the salvation of the world mandates our separation from all other churches. Please consider these two next statements:

Remember, there is no other church or group of people anywhere in this world that understands what the messages of the three angels are! Not one! Once again, it is the Spirit of Prophecy that reveals its own need to the people of God. If we refuse to seek the counsel God has given His denominated people through Inspiration, we will find ourselves deceived in the end, for it is those who refuse "to heed the warnings God has given" (*Selected Messages*, book 1, 200), that fall into the final deceptions coming upon the world. We must stand for the truth and "meet" head on any deceptions threatening to impair or undermine the giving of the three angels' messages: "If unity could be secured only by the compromise of

6 Alberto R. Treiyer, *Seals & Trumpets: Biblical and Historical Studies*. Ooltewah, TN: Adventist Distinctive Messages, 2005, 372, 373.

truth and righteousness, then let there be difference, *and even war"(The Great Controversy*, 1888 ed., 45, emphasis added).

At times, "war" is the only choice that will dispel the darkness. So let it be! It is essential that we understand how God has called the Seventh-day Adventist Church to proclaim "the most solemn, sacred work ever given to mortals," and as long as we continue to flirt and sleep with the fallen daughters of Babylon, we will never succeed in enlightening the world with this message. Such a union will only hinder the giving of "the most solemn, sacred work" (*Manuscript Releases*, vol. 7, 105).

Seventh-day Adventists have believed for 150 years that the "beast" that comes up out of the earth represents the United States of America and it is Protestant America that "causeth" the earth and those who live there to worship the first beast of Revelation 13, Roman Catholicism. It somehow compels the entire world to worship papal Rome. Also, as Adventists, we have shown how the Spirit of Prophecy, commenting on Scripture, supports the fact that the Roman Catholic system will eventually control the entire world. Now let us look at Scripture.

> The ten horns which thou sawest are ten kings, which have received no kingdom as yet; but receive power as kings one hour with the beast. These have one mind, and shall give their power and strength unto the beast. These shall make war with the Lamb, and the Lamb shall overcome them: for he is Lord of lords, and King of kings: and they that are with him are called, and chosen, and faithful. And he saith unto me, The waters which thou sawest, where the whore sitteth, are peoples, and multitudes, and nations, and tongues. And the ten horns which thou sawest upon the beast, these shall hate the whore, and shall make her desolate and naked, and shall eat her flesh, and burn her with fire. For God hath put in their hearts to fulfil his will, and to agree, and give their kingdom unto the beast, until the words of God shall be fulfilled. And the woman which thou sawest is that great city, which reigneth over the kings of the earth. (Revelation 17:12–18)

These are the final movements of the nations on earth. Ten (being the number of the world) represents all the kingdoms of the world, and Scripture says they "have one mind, and shall give their power and strength to the beast" (Revelation 17:13). In the Greek, the word translated as "power" is appropriate, but the English term "strength," *ἐξουσία*

(*Strong's* G1849), translated as "power of choice," is used only this one time in the entire New Testament. It is more meaningful if another English term, "authority," is also considered as it is used 29 other times. The word "strength" implies a meaning similar to "power," but adding the concept of "authority" is helpful in understanding where the strength is coming from. Other uses or definitions of this word include "power" 69 times, "authority" 29 times, "right" two times, and "jurisdiction" and "liberty" each one time (*Strong's Exhaustive Concordance*, 1996 ed.). The *Strong's* definitions III and IV for authority are:

III. the power of authority (influence) and of right (privilege)

IV. the power of rule or government (the power of him whose will and commands must be submitted to by others and obeyed)

- A. universally
  - i. authority over mankind
- B. specifically
  - i. the power of judicial decisions
  - ii. of authority to manage domestic affairs
- C. metonymically
  - i. a thing subject to authority or rule
    - a. a jurisdiction
  - ii. one who possesses authority

So these worldly powers choose to submit themselves by giving their authority to rule and to judge to the beast power to decide for them what is proper morally. This brings up the question concerning the meaning of "mind" where Scripture says that these kings have "one mind." What could this mean?

The Greek word *γνώμη* (*Strong's* G1106) is translated as "judgment" three times, "mind" twice, "purpose" once, "advice" once, "will" once, and "agree" once. The *Strong's* definitions for mind are:

I. the faculty of knowledge, mind, reason

II. that which is thought or known; one's mind

- A. view, judgment, opinion

B. mind concerning what ought to be done
   i. by one's self: resolve purpose, intention
   ii. by others: judgment, advice
   iii. decree

So one could say that the kingdoms of this world come to a place where the leadership of all the individual nations seems to think alike and have the same goals, purposes, and intentions, are of the same judgment and opinion, and are prepared to agree on the same actions for the future. Additionally, Revelation chapter 18 contains the information needed to understand why the "kings of the earth," represented by those "ten kings," decided to give themselves over to Rome, "that great city, which reigneth over the kings of the earth" (Revelation 17:18).

It is implied that the merchants and great men of the world became rich and lived "deliciously" in this world because of their inappropriate relationship with Rome, described by the words "the kings of the earth, who have committed fornication and lived deliciously with her" (Revelation 18:9). What kind of relationship between the "merchants" and "great men" of the earth and Roman Catholicism is described in these verses? Since the merchants and great men of the world are those who control the world, obviously, this is where Rome has her influence in making globalization a reality.

It is not my purpose to attempt to describe how all these things will take place, only that they will. Scripture and the Spirit of Prophecy support this teaching.

This is Bible truth. So who can argue that when the entire world is brought under a certain type of global control it will be that much easier for Roman Catholicism, the power moving behind the scenes and that comes "up out of the abyss" (Revelation 17:8, NIV), to have a much easier time being the moral authority such a system will need? This is a position we know she is destined to fill.

We are told that if we desire to understand how these things are going to take place, all we need do is search past history and discover the methods that Rome used in the past to accomplish this same thing. God has supplied His remnant people with the Inspiration needed to study past history with an accuracy we can rely on—another reason for us to use this precious gift.

In the next few paragraphs is a most important concept, summarizing certain ideas that, when considered together, will define the tremendous danger of what is being presented to the Seventh-day Adventist Church by those who have been affected by emergent theology. Jesus allowed this movement to manifest itself, but that does not mean it is the truth or it has His blessing, for we have been warned that the Lord would allow false teachings to infiltrate the church to bring about the shaking. This is why we believe this movement exists. Every one of us must determine the source behind this movement and others that will arise in the future, whether they have God's blessing or not. How are we to do this?

Our only guide is the Holy Spirit in our hearts, working through Scripture and the Spirit of Prophecy. Directing our people to these two sources when judging all teachings is a primary objective of both this book and *The Omega Rebellion*. It is why both are filled with quotes from these sources. These books are not just my ideas, but are the result of studying the inspired writings God has given His church in the context of the teachings being analyzed. You might say that the homework has been done for those who will have to study for themselves and make a choice. Gathered together are words from the pen of Inspiration, attempting to maintain the proper context and applying them to the teachings of the emerging church. Consideration of the history of these movements, and to a certain extent the people behind them, round out this study.

Now you, my Adventist family, can study what has been put together and make your own decisions. Are they from God and meant to bring a great revival, or are they the counterfeit we have been warned about? To find the truth, we need to humbly continue to study those same inspired writings that warned us of the counterfeit in the first place, Scripture and the Spirit of Prophecy. Those involved in the practice of spiritual formation and who are followers of the emerging church seem to avoid and ignore these writings when presented to them. Yet within these very writings lie the greatest clue to where the truth will be found.

Isn't it true that the Jesuits have prided themselves on their unique sense of brotherhood, a bond existing through their education and sworn purpose for existence, being willing even to die for their cause? Now, please consider the following ideas carefully.

We need to look at what is happening currently, now, today. Europe is emerging as a united empire under the leadership of Rome. The Vatican has been working toward this goal for centuries, for the papacy must be in control of a united Europe before it can fulfill its lifelong desire to rule the world. We know from Scripture that it will succeed, for the whole world will worship the beast when its deadly wound is healed. We are simply observing current events to see where we are in history and how close we are to the fulfillment of these events. God's method for answering these questions is to investigate prophecy.

Rome is very patient and carefully plans her course, striking only when she is sure to succeed. Little by little, she has been constructing a plan to become the moral and political leader of the world. She is secretly behind all the unusual movements in Europe that seem haphazard and coincidental. They are neither, but instead are the results of working behind the scenes to bring a united Europe into reality, with the papacy being the moral leader who will control its future. Then, with the weakening of the economies of the superpowers of the world and the crisis which will arise, the world will plead for her intervention and leadership. She is setting the stage for all these things to occur now. Read on.

At a recent meeting of The Pontifical Council for Justice and Peace, (Address of His Holiness Pope Benedict XVI to participants in the Plenary Assembly of the Pontifical Council for Justice and Peace, 3 December 2012) Pope Benedict XVI called for the world to look for a political and moral power, to which it could look for counsel, leadership, and control of the complex future of a globalized society and economy. He said neither the United Nations, nor any superpower, could fill the position because of their selfish motives. They needed a moral leader, and the United Nations has shown many times over that it fails in this respect; as for any nation filling the position, they would be influenced by their own self-seeking political aims and desires. No, this power needs to be one that is respected by the world as a moral leader, that will judge fairly, and that will not have the political and economic interests of individual nations in mind.

Benedict was, without doubt, baiting the world to choose the Roman Catholic Church to fill that role, without ever having to name the church of which he was the head. He expressed the same thoughts in an encyclical he wrote in 2009. It will be worth reading some of what he said and applying his words to Revelation 18 and the illicit relationship Rome will have with the "merchants, and the great and mighty men" of the earth at the time of the end:

> The following quotation is taken from:
>
> ENCYCLICAL LETTER CARITAS IN VERITATE
> OF THE SUPREME PONTIFF BENEDICT XVI TO THE BISHOPS
>
> 66. Global interconnectedness has led to the emergence of a new political power, that of consumers and their associations. This is a

phenomenon that needs to be further explored, as it contains positive elements to be encouraged as well as excesses to be avoided. It is good for people to realize that purchasing is always a moral—and not simply economic—act. Hence the consumer has a specific social responsibility, which goes hand-in- hand with the social responsibility of the enterprise… it can be helpful to promote new ways of marketing products from deprived areas of the world, so as to guarantee their producers a decent return. However, certain conditions need to be met: the market should be genuinely transparent; the producers, as well as increasing their profit margins, should also receive improved formation in professional skills and technology. …

67. *In the face of the unrelenting growth of global interdependence, there is a strongly felt need, even in the midst of a global recession, for a reform of the United Nations Organization,* and likewise of economic institutions and international finance, *so that the concept of the family of nations can acquire real teeth.* One also senses the urgent need to find innovative ways of implementing the principle of the responsibility to protect [146] and of giving poorer nations an effective voice in shared decision-making. This seems necessary in order to arrive at a political, juridical and economic order which can increase and give direction to international cooperation for the development of all peoples in solidarity. To manage the global economy; to revive economies hit by the crisis; to avoid any deterioration of the present crisis and the greater imbalances that would result; to bring about integral and timely disarmament, food security and peace; to guarantee the protection of the environment and to regulate migration: *for all this, there is urgent need of a true world political authority, as my predecessor Blessed John XXIII indicated some years ago.* Such an authority would need to be regulated by law, to observe consistently the principles of subsidiarity and solidarity, to seek to establish the common good[147], and to make a commitment to securing authentic integral human development inspired by the values of charity in truth. *Furthermore, such an authority would need to be universally recognized and to be vested with the effective power to ensure security for all, regard for justice, and respect for rights* [148]. Obviously it would have to have the authority to ensure compliance with its decisions from all parties, and also with the coordinated measures adopted in various international forums. Without this, despite the great progress accomplished in various sectors, international law

> would risk being conditioned by the balance of power among the strongest nations. The integral development of peoples and international cooperation require the establishment of a greater degree of international ordering, marked by subsidiarity. They also require the construction of a social order that at last conforms to the moral order, to the interconnection between moral and social spheres, and to the link between politics and the economic and civil spheres, as envisaged by the Charter of the United Nations.

There is no doubt that the papacy is the only worldwide voice and power that could possibly fill the shoes of the power described in these words. This is where we are headed and these are the plans for the future that the Church of Rome has for herself. Consider seriously that these are the words of a "church." Have you ever heard words like this coming from any other "church" in this world? "No," must be your answer, and that is because we are not dealing with just a church, but with the beast of Revelation Chapter 13, the antichrist whose destiny is to control the world for a short time before Jesus returns! This will happen, my friends, and the Lord has raised our church to warn the world of these things through our "most solemn" message.

The Jesuits have a great amount of control among the European nations, working behind the scenes. They control banking systems, economies, and the administration of nations. Three of the largest and most powerful nations in the European Union are led either from the top or have leaders sympathetic to Roman Catholicism. A group exists of leaders who hold positions from presidents to prime ministers, to economic banking secretaries, and consider themselves part of a "club" consisting of those with Jesuit roots—that is, those who have graduated from Jesuit colleges or who are themselves Jesuits. They speak outwardly of their common heritage and brotherhood, and have openly declared that they have this bond and all agree when it comes to the future of Europe. These folks have been sharing responsibilities and leadership in many of the secretive organizations, such as the Trilateral Commission, and have been consistently in and out of the Vatican where they meet with leading officials and with the pope himself. Now, in the latest development, the Roman Catholic Church has, for the first time in its history, elected a Jesuit to be its new leader, Pope Francis.

Could it be possible that the influence of supernatural power upon many people through techniques invented by the Jesuits in the disciplines taught by the emerging church, along with the Jesuits' infiltration into the affairs of nations via positions of leadership and political authority, is the how and why the nations of this world become of "one mind"? Consider this: it has been reported by Keep the Faith Ministry that the leading Roman Catholic politicians in the nations of Europe have been informed that in order for the European Union to succeed, Ignatian spirituality must be practiced. My fellow Adventist, please consider what you have just read. What could be the reason for such counsel, other than the satanic mind control of people holding key positions in the nations of Europe?

Think about the control and influence that Satan has upon the people who practice his disciplines, having the opposite results of those who surrender to God. Satan binds his followers together, and the Holy Spirit binds together those who follow Jesus. Scripture says, "Let this mind be in you" (Philippians 2:5) in reference to the mind of Christ. Contrarily, those who have surrendered to Satan by rejecting godly counsel and refusing to "heed the warnings God has given" (*The Review and Herald*, December 4, 1900), and follow the spiritualistic methods of the emerging church, have actually surrendered themselves to the mind of Satan. Without knowing it, they are hypnotized as was Eve in the Garden of Eden. She had been talking with Satan, thinking it was an intelligent serpent.

Those who practice Ignatian spirituality are also talking with Satan although they believe they have entered into the presence of God. Others, who have been instructed by emerging church teachers and mentors from the fallen churches and their universities, also believe they are listening to God's instruction when in reality it is the same power that was behind the serpent's voice in the Garden of Eden. They are deceived because they have rejected God's counsel and will not heed the warnings God gives us.

Listening to error when we have received inspired warnings not to listen ends in demonic control and hypnosis. In God's remarkable way, He speaks and dwells in the hearts of His followers, and through the supernatural power of hypnosis, Satan dwells in the hearts of those who are deceived and have rejected God, following him instead. So the mind of Jesus dwells within His followers and the mind of Satan within his.

The Bible verse in Revelation 17 that says the kings of the earth have "one mind" may now have more meaning than before, understanding the supernatural methods used by Satan to control those whom he has deceived. Inspiration confirms that these events will occur; also, do not forget that the Jesuits invented the theology and discipline used in spiritual formation and in the emergent church.

We can see globalism's political agenda at work in the midst of these final movements and watch the merchants of the earth and the great men of the world—the leaders of nations, having their minds drawn together toward the "one mind" as they work toward gathering the entire world under Roman authority. It is happening now, and it is astonishing. These merchants and great men have lined up and joined forces with Rome, eager to accept the benefits of their adulterous relationship. Here is commentary from *The Great Controversy*:

> A profession of religion has become popular with the world. Rulers, politicians, lawyers, doctors, merchants, join the church as a means of securing the respect and confidence of society, and advancing their own worldly interests. Thus they seek to cover all their unrighteous transactions under a profession of Christianity. The various religious bodies, re-enforced by the wealth and influence of these baptized worldlings, make a still higher bid for popularity and patronage. Splendid churches, embellished in the most extravagant manner, are erected on popular avenues. The worshipers array themselves in costly and fashionable attire. A high salary is paid for a talented minister to entertain and attract the people. His sermons must not touch popular sins, but be made smooth and pleasing for fashionable ears. Thus fashionable sinners are enrolled on the church-records, and fashionable sins are concealed under a pretense of godliness. "The merchants of the earth," that have "waxed rich through the abundance of her delicacies," "shall stand afar off for the fear of her torment, weeping and wailing, and saying, Alas, alas that great city, that was clothed in fine linen, and purple, and scarlet, and decked with gold, and precious stones, and pearls! For in one hour so great riches is come to nought." Revelation 18:11, 3, 15–17. (*The Great Controversy*, 653)

Ecumenism

Satan is well aware that anything he can do to prevent the Seventh-day Adventist Church from understanding and taking the proper steps to fulfill her mission prolongs the time until his final demise. He is gaining ground whenever the leaders of our church cooperate in any way with the evangelical Protestant churches and their desire to unite upon common teachings. Look at what Ellen White wrote about this threat in her day, more than 100 years ago:

> The wide diversity of belief in the Protestant churches is regarded by many as decisive proof that no effort to secure a forced uniformity can ever be made. But there has been for years, in churches of the Protestant faith, a strong and growing sentiment in favor of a union based upon common points of doctrine. To secure such a union, the discussion of subjects upon which all were not agreed—however important they might be from a Bible standpoint—must necessarily be waived.
>
> Charles Beecher, in a sermon in the year 1846, declared that the ministry of "the evangelical Protestant denominations" is "not only formed all the way up under a tremendous pressure of merely human fear, but they live, and move, and breathe in a state of things radically corrupt, and appealing every hour to every baser element of their nature to hush up the truth, and bow the knee to the power of apostasy. Was not this the way things went with Rome? Are we not living her life over again? And what do we see just ahead? Another general council! A world's convention! Evangelical alliance, and universal creed!"—Sermon on "The Bible a Sufficient Creed," delivered at Fort Wayne, Indiana, Feb. 22, 1846. When this shall be gained, then, in the effort to secure complete uniformity, it will be only a step to the resort to force. (*The Great Controversy*, 444, 445)

Then Ellen White penned these prophetic words:

> When the leading churches of the United States, uniting upon such points of doctrine as are held by them in common, shall influence the state to enforce their decrees and to sustain their institutions, then Protestant America will have formed an image of the Roman hierarchy, and the infliction of civil penalties upon dissenters will inevitably result. (*The Great Controversy*, 445)

The emerging church movement is designed to draw the Protestant churches together under the teachings and beliefs of Roman Catholicism, for they are the founders of the spiritualistic teachings, basic to the emergent church movement—"Ignatian spirituality." One of the goals of this emergent movement is to break down the barriers that exist between the Protestant churches and unify them globally—the very motive Ellen White said existed among the evangelical churches. This is the prerequisite to the formation of the persecuting "image of the beast." Please think about this point and how it relates to emergent church teachings within God's church.

To conclude this chapter, we need to understand the overwhelming power in Roman Catholic theology and why the fallen human nature is so easily attracted to it. The power of Catholicism's theology is that it supplies Christians with a belief system promising that they can continually enjoy the sin in this world and still have access to the eternal joy of heaven. The comfort for those who do not believe that we are under the authority of God's law is that forgiveness for whatever is their concept of sin is as close as the priest's confessional, and that no change or repentance is needed. This belief system contains no moral restraints and gives the follower the freedom to continue to behave the same as before, and like the Jesuits, they live by the motto that the end justifies the means.

The church's influence over its 1.2 billion members all over the world tends to feed the fallen desires for power and materialism, the greatest gifts this world has to offer its merchants and great men. The result for those who are a part of this system is as the Spirit of Prophecy claims, "They had neglected to feed the hungry, to clothe the naked, to deal justly, and to love mercy. They had sought to exalt themselves and to obtain the homage of their fellow creatures" (*The Great Controversy*, 654)—all this while deceiving the world into believing that these very things are its real purpose.

This is life without a real relationship with God—one that trusts in the priest's power of forgiveness. There are few restraints or requirements in such a system aside from performing the sacraments and accepting the supposed grace they offer. When one feels the need, simply do the work—no repentance necessary. This is not true religion, it does not change the heart, and it results in the selfishness that identifies the merchants and great men described in Revelation 18.

Simply put, Satan's antichrist masterpiece that we call Roman Catholicism teaches its believers that it is possible to enjoy all the sin this fallen world has to offer and still have the approval of God through the practice of confession. So Scripture appropriately calls this satanic masterpiece that is about to take control of the entire world the "man of sin" and "the mystery of iniquity" (2 Thessalonians 2:3, 7).

Chapter Five:

From Alpha to Omega

It has been more than 100 years since the alpha apostasy of Dr. John Harvey Kellogg and his book *The Living Temple* was published. More than eleven decades have passed since Dr. Kellogg wrote *The Living Temple*, and Ellen White warned us of the omega apostasy to come.

Throughout our history, numerous movements have been pointed out as possible "omega" apostasies. Many times, voices have arisen, warning the church of present-day deceptions. Obviously, since they have come and gone, they were not fulfillments of the final deception, although they were definitely individual cars in that "train of deception" called the omega.

Our General Conference president gave us just such a warning in his Sabbath sermon on the 3rd of July 2010. In that message the newly elected General Conference president, Elder Ted N. C. Wilson advised the church:

> Don't reach out to movements or mega church centers outside the Seventh-day Adventist Church which promise you spiritual success based on faulty theology. Stay away from non-biblical spiritual disciplines or methods of spiritual formation that are rooted in mysticism such as contemplative prayer, centering prayer, and the emerging church movement in which they are promoted. Look WITHIN the Seventh-day Adventist Church to humble pastors, evangelists, Biblical scholars, leaders, and departmental directors who can provide evangelistic methods and programs that are based on solid Biblical principles and "The Great Controversy Theme."[7]

Recently, the Biblical Research Institute reviewed a book called *The Green Cord Dream*, which many believe contains the heresy of the omega.

---

7 Ted N. C. Wilson's sermon, "Go Forward," at the General Conference Session, Atlanta, GA, July 3, 2010.

The Biblical Research Institute did not feel they could endorse the book entirely, stating that *The Green Cord Dream* is liable to leave a "skewed picture" of the Adventist church. Specific concerns mentioned included the encouragement of ecumenism, the blurring of doctrinal distinctives, and an "implied denigration of the Adventist Church and its teachings.[8]

Only time will tell, of course, if the teachings of the emerging church in the movements now affecting Adventism are actually the "omega," but they contain enough that we know to be error that we need to look carefully at their movements within God's church.

Spiritual formation is a satanic deception, structured upon Jesuit pantheistic spirituality. Its planned use, as we have already discovered, is that it be the primary tool used by the Roman Catholic Church to regain control of the world, while concurrently counteracting the worldwide mission of the Seventh-day Adventist Church. Please take note that spiritual formation, Ignatian spirituality, and contemplative spirituality are all terms denoting the same practices and disciplines. Here are a few statements out of the instruction to the church from Vatican II: Mission of the Catholic Church, Decree *Ad Gentes*, On The Mission Activity of the Church.

> Institutes of the contemplative life, by their prayers, sufferings, and works of penance have a very great importance in the conversion of souls. … In fact, these institutes are asked to found houses in mission areas, as not a few of them have already done, so that there, living out their lives in a way accommodated to the truly religious traditions of the people, they can bear excellent witness among non-Christians to the majesty and love of God, as well as to our union in Christ. …
>
> Worthy of special mention are the various projects for causing the contemplative life to take root …
>
> Since the contemplative life belongs to the fullness of the Church's presence, let it be put into effect everywhere. Religious institutes of the contemplative and of the active life, have so far played, and still do play, the main role in the evangelization of the world.

---

8 Gerhard Pfandl, "Book Notes on *The Green Cord Dream*," *Reflections*, no. 42, newsletter of the Biblical Research Institute (April 2013),https://www.uccsda.org/files/communications/2013%20BRI%20newsltr%204-13%20%28%2342%29.pdf (accessed January 27, 2014).

Again:
...the main role in the evangelization of the world.

This is most significant news for Seventh-day Adventists, clarifying our understanding of exactly how the papacy plans to entice the entire world to worship at its altar. These are the means through which it plans to accomplish the very thing we have been warning the world of for 150 years. Read the following very carefully, for it concerns current preparations for this world's final crisis, events predicted in Scripture and the Spirit of Prophecy that must occur in both spiritual and political arenas.

We have provided evidence from the writings of Vatican II that the "contemplative life" consists of mystical teachings learned in the discipline called "spiritual formation." The claim is made that these teachings belong to the Roman Catholic Church and should be put into practice everywhere in order to evangelize the whole world. Included therein are the dangers of mysticism in the practice of visiting the "silence," an altered state of consciousness resulting from the practice of what is called "contemplative prayer," the type of prayer that lies at the heart of spiritual formation teachings. This is the prayer that functionally opens the doorway of the mind to the supernatural at the specific time desired. However, by practicing any part of spiritual formation teachings, participants place themselves under satanic control, for this entire discipline is based on the supernatural revelations Satan gave to Ignatius Loyola.

Special Note: There is no question that the power behind the development of every facet of spiritual formation, including those apart from the "silence" and "contemplative prayer," is satanic. The entire teaching is a mixture of truth and error. There are surely true and proper practices, but they are mixed with error. This forces the Seventh-day Adventist student to attempt to discern between the two, something we show to be unattainable because it requires the rejection of inspired counsel. God has instructed us to refuse even to listen to teachers who mix truth and error. I pray you see the point. (See Chapter Three: Warnings.)

With regard to these future plans of the papacy, and its plans for the use of spiritual formation, consider this: the altered states associated with the "silence" and "contemplative prayer" are not our only concern. Think carefully of what we as God's remnant church are doing when we go outside our church to learn the teachings of spiritual formation, knowing we have been warned against it. This teaching has emerged from the depths of hell—Roman Catholic Jesuitism—and it is not only the mystical teachings that are dangerous, but the entire process comes from Satan's army of Jesuit elites.

There are dynamics at play of which we all need to be aware. Eve fell under the hypnotic influence of Satan without having to perform any mind-altering gymnastics. She did not have to "center" her mind through a learned technique, or prayer. She did not need to study Ignatian spirituality or contemplative prayer. All she did was reject God's warnings and then converse with the devil. This is extremely important to understand, and we need to investigate Inspiration further. We read:

> Our first parents were not left without a warning of the danger that threatened them [in the Garden of Eden]. (*Patriarchs and Prophets*, 52)

> I saw that the holy angels often visited the garden, and gave instruction to Adam and Eve concerning their employment, and also taught them concerning the rebellion of Satan and his fall. The angels warned them of Satan, and cautioned them not to separate from each other in their employment, for they might be brought in contact with this fallen foe. The angels enjoined upon them to closely follow the directions God had given them, for in perfect obedience only were they safe. And if they were obedient, this fallen foe could have no power over them. (*Spiritual Gifts*, vols. 1 and 2, 20)

> The angels warned them to be on their guard against the devices of Satan, for his efforts to ensnare them would be unwearied. While they were obedient to God the evil one could not harm them; for, if need be, every angel in heaven would be sent to their help. If they steadfastly repelled his first insinuations, they would be as secure as the heavenly messengers. But should they once yield to temptation, their nature would become so depraved that in themselves they would have no power and no disposition to resist Satan.
>
> The tree of knowledge had been made a test of their obedience and their love to God. The Lord had seen fit to lay upon them but one prohibition as to the use of all that was in the garden; but if they should disregard His will in this particular, they would incur the

> guilt of transgression. Satan was not to follow them with continual temptations; he could have access to them only at the forbidden tree. Should they attempt to investigate its nature, they would be exposed to his wiles. They were admonished to give careful heed to the warning which God had sent them and to be content with the instruction which He had seen fit to impart. (*Patriarch and Prophets,* 53)

Eve's resistance to following instruction was enough for Satan to gain control of her mind. Why? Eve refused to "give careful heed to the warning" God gave her, and because of this, Satan had the right to hypnotize her. Eve fell under Satan's power because she chose to disregard God's counsel, choosing Satan instead of God. We are in the exact same position Eve was in when we disregard God's counsel and go to learn spiritual formation, or for that matter, any other teaching where truth is mixed with error, believing we can discern truth from error. If we do this, we will be deceived and will fall under Satan's hypnotic power even though nothing that we would recognize as supernatural needs to take place.

We are deceiving ourselves if we believe that we have the ability to discern truth from error and accept only the "good" parts of their teachings, as so many Adventists claim they do when attending schools of the fallen churches. Many point to the fact that we teach these subjects at the seminary and point to how many other Seventh-day Adventists have attended the same schools they attended and read the same books.

These excuses do nothing more than condemn others along with themselves of violating the counsel we have in the Spirit of Prophecy. Inspiration clearly teaches us that we are unable to discern what is "good" because we have fallen under the control of demonic power through our choice to violate God's instruction and warnings. This places us in the frightening position where fallen angels have the right to control us. We have driven away the only source of our protection, the angels God commissioned to protect us. We have the Catholic Church's own admission and claim that this teaching is theirs and that they plan to use it to control the world, bringing everyone they can back to the Catholic Church. We ask, "Where are our sensibilities?" Again, he is sparing no person, no church, least of all ours.

Why would he give the Adventist church a "pass," allowing us to conduct our business unimpeded? If not alert, we can be pacified into waiting for the familiarity of "end-time troubles," thinking our adversary's interest is more minimal now than it will be in the future. Alert, vigilantly attentive, mentally responsive, and perceptive are the characteristics that must be applied to the testing of unique and distinct teachings that enter the church. It is the concern that, upon examination, The One Project is one of these to be carefully questioned for its veracity and its consequence.

It is now the concern of many as well as the premise of this book that the roots of The One Project are harbored within the Jesuit arm of Roman Catholicism as expressed through its infiltration of Protestantism via the emerging church movement. It is directly connected to our leading institutions of higher learning by men who have been formally trained in this Roman discipline. The One Project teachings as well as *The Green Cord Dream*, a book which provides the basis of The One Project teaching, reveal the direct influence by prominent leaders of the emerging church movement. One of these prominent figures, Dr. Leonard Sweet, is noted as one of the most influential Christian leaders in America; he is often listed within the top ten. Dr. Sweet currently holds positions as the E. Stanley Jones Professor of Evangelism at Drew Theological School at Drew University in Madison, New Jersey. He is also a distinguished visiting professor at George Fox University in Portland, Oregon. As noted, four of the five co-founders of The One Project received their doctorate degrees in leadership and emerging culture, a course of study in which the school says Dr. Sweet is the official mentor.

In chapter eight, we will analyze the book *The Green Cord Dream* as well as the theology presented by the author. We will address his theology, comparing it with Scripture and the Spirit of Prophecy. Of interest to note, a copy of the book, *I Am a Follower: The Way, Truth, and Life of Following Jesus*, by Christian mystic Dr. Leonard Sweet, was distributed at The One Project's Seattle meeting.

Of interest also is that most of the leaders in the Seventh-day Adventist Church who are actively supporting and advancing this new movement, including all of those who founded it, have been strong advocates and promoters of the teachings of emergent theology and spiritual formation. As mentioned, spiritual formation is a Roman Catholic teaching planned to be used to win the world back to their worship community. Its central purpose and the source of its effectiveness is Satan's hypnotic power, or going right to the bottom line, spiritualism. The entire discipline, even apart from the supernatural altered states of consciousness like those of contemplative and centering prayer, is based upon the satanically-inspired spiritual exercises of Ignatius Loyola, (founder of the Jesuit Order) and is what makes the discipline so dangerous.

There is no excuse for any Seventh-day Adventist to practice any part of this discipline, with or without its contemplative components, for all of it is Roman Catholic and has been created for the purpose of winning over the entire world to papal control. God called the Seventh-day Adventist Church to warn the world of these very teachings. Many involved have become so blind that they can no longer discern truth from error. Still, there are many who are not totally resistant to the truth, and they can and will respond to our prayers—their condition is not incurable—"buy of me gold, tried in the fire" (Revelation 3:18). The Holy Spirit of truth is the cure and is the reason for this book. You must be the judge.

Another point to be made is that every component of the teaching called spiritual formation is meant to improve the spiritual life and comes from Babylon, which means our acceptance of any of those components from their teachings violates the counsels we have been specifically given. Please consider this point—no element of this teaching should be considered or accepted in God's remnant church, even if we agree with it. It is impossible for us to discern truth from error if we approach these teachings desiring to discover light and truth. We will become confused, and this is the reason for not accepting any part of it even if we know its truth. We must find that truth in what God has given us, not in teachings that contain truth mixed with error. Why? It is as we already pointed out:

> If God has any new light to communicate, He will let His chosen and beloved understand it, without their going to have their minds enlightened by hearing those who are in darkness and error." (*Early Writings*, 124)

The Seventh-day Adventist Church has in many ways fallen from following the Lord's inspired counsel and it has become fashionable for us to seek the knowledge of the fallen churches and bring their teachings home—e.g., Willow Creek. This does not mean that it is the correct thing to do. It is far worse to ignore the inspired instruction that warned against this activity than if we did not have it in the first place.

Spiritual formation, a supposed benign practice to advance one's spiritual life, is being encouraged and taught in a number of our schools. In many cases these theories are believed in and practiced by those who go on to join and support the theology of The One Project, which fundamentally teaches the doctrine of the emerging church. The book *The Green Cord Dream* is filled with recommendations to read authors steeped in emergent theology, namely Manning, Clairborne, Nouwen, and others. There are surely true and proper practices contained in this discipline, but they are mixed with mystical error, forcing Seventh-day Adventist students to attempt to discern between the two, something we show to be unattainable because it requires the rejection of inspired counsel. As already pointed out, God has instructed us to refuse even to listen to teachers who mix truth and error, without His specific leading to do it. We pray that you are beginning to see the point. To repeat, from the counsel we have, none of these teachings should be searched through in order to discover new light (see Isaiah 8:20).

To be specific, the silence is outright hypnotism, with demons involved in mind control and illusion. The rest is a mixture of truth and error, which we are instructed to avoid in our search for truth and light. The entire discipline of the silence or contemplative prayer is Satan's spiritualism, and because of our insistence in practicing something we have been warned to stay clear of, we fall under the satanic power of the prince of evil. Whether we are aware of it or not, by this practice we counteract the work of the Holy Spirit in God's remnant church.

Satan counterfeits the Holy Spirit with spiritualistic power, controlling the minds of his people. This is a very real power. The true Holy Spirit directs the minds of God's people. Satan is using his power to influence those who have been deceived. In ways that only the Holy Spirit understands, He works with those under His control in God's church. Satan controls who he can with an enticing and powerful deception, counterfeiting the work of the Holy Spirit.

Why are some deceived into agreeing with these new teachings? As the remnant church, we have an accurate understanding of Scripture and the inspired writings of Ellen White as a guide to follow all the way into the kingdom of God. It seems that it must be the lack of understanding of the truths God has especially blessed our church with. When we ignore truth and refuse to heed the warnings God has given in the Spirit of Prophecy, what more can He do to save us? He will not force us. These actions permit evil angels to influence our minds, forcing the heavenly angels who watch over us to retreat. These "evil angels are upon our track every moment" (*Testimonies for the Church*, vol. 1, 302).When we deny, ignore, or refuse to follow the truth from inspired sources, we are choosing to allow them to have hypnotic control over us. It is so sad and so simple, and is all about choice, God's greatest gift to mankind. Here is God's counsel:

> Just as long as men consent to listen to these sophistries, a subtle influence will weave the fine threads of these seductive theories into their minds, and men who should turn away from the first sound of such teaching will learn to love it. As loyal subjects we must refuse even to listen to these sophistries. Their influence is something like a deadly viper, poisoning the minds of all who listen. It is a branch of hypnotism, deadening the sensibilities of the soul. (*Manuscript Releases*, vol. 10, 163)

Here is the problem—in his rebuttal, (Epilogue #2) when explaining the use and recommendation of authors in his book *The Green Cord Dream, Dr. Bryan indicated that he did not believe everything they believed, but that he selects only those teachings that comport with Seventh-day Adventist belief.*

It seems he has fallen into the same trap that all who study these books for spiritual growth, or to find some light therein, fall into. It is one thing to read material from the authors of the fallen churches for research and other kinds of educational purposes, but it violates God's counsel to read it with the intent to separate the truth from the error in order to discover the light it contains. From what has been written in *The Green Cord Dream*, he has obviously accepted many teachings that do not "comport with the fundamental beliefs of the Seventh-day Adventist Church."

He points out how he has applied the teachings from books that have been written by mystics and spiritualists to his own life. He believes in those books and recommends them to all who will listen. These are teachers who mix truth and error. Gerhard Pfandl, who reviewed *The Green Cord Dream* for the Biblical Research Institute (BRI), made this statement, "*The Green Cord Dream* is a book that will primarily appeal to young Adventists, and therein lies its danger." (*Reflections*, BRI Newsletter 4/13, #42)[9]

What is the danger? It is the same danger that resulted in the acceptance of dangerous teachings by the author and the movement's leaders. Once again, Dr. Bryan's claim is made, "I critically read and scrutinize all material to comport with the fundamental beliefs of the Seventh-day Adventist Church." He may critically read and scrutinize, but if we are to

9 Pfandl, *Reflections.*

believe the inspiration of the Spirit of Prophecy, it cannot do him any good, and he deceives himself, for Inspiration says:

> Just as long as men consent to listen to these sophistries, a subtle influence will weave the fine threads of these seductive theories into their minds, and men who should turn away from the first sound of such teaching will learn to love it. As loyal subjects we must refuse even to listen to these sophistries. Their influence is something like a deadly viper, poisoning the minds of all who listen. It is a branch of hypnotism, deadening the sensibilities of the soul. (*Manuscript Releases*, vol. 10, 163)

Notice how it says that they "will learn to love it" as a consequence of specious teachings. Is the experience of joy, relief, peace, adventure, emotion, and passion a good indicator as to whether or not a teaching is true? Tracking roots and understanding origins is the key to answering this question. We are told that demons stand by the side of those sitting at the feet of the teachers of Babylon—fulfilling the conditions that Inspiration speaks of often—the development of hypnotism and deception.

The fact that others in God's church have made the same choice does not change anything. Some may think they are knowledgeable enough to discern truth from error, but Inspiration disagrees. It is not a question of how much truth we know; it is a question of which supernatural powers are influencing us. We're told that God's angels must back away and allow fallen angels to take their places. This is the consequence of the actions taken by those who sat at the feet of the teachers from George Fox University and other schools. Those students believe they have learned wonderful new truths and have learned to love this "new light." In reality it is not light, but darkness; the same deception that captured Dr. Kellogg in the alpha apostasy, and those conditions we are told will be repeated near the end of time. Is this what we are witnessing, and is this why the book, *The Green Cord Dream*, is filled with the deceptive ideas and teachings of those in the emerging church? Remember, the BRI says there is "an implied denigration of the Adventist church and its teachings." [10]

Next, let us consider those who actually practice centering and contemplative prayer. They tend to believe that they can communicate with Jesus through the disciplines learned in spiritual formation. This practice

---

10 Ibid.

brings them under the influence of demons. Furthermore, they are taught a pantheistic Christology, claiming that Jesus in His fullness can be found in every human being, and, some even believe, in all of His creation. It is sad indeed that their only hope is found in the very counsel that they have failed to investigate before accepting this false theology. Here are a few of those warnings:

> It introduces that which is nought but speculation in regard to the personality of God and where His presence is. No one on this earth has a right to speculate on this question. (*Selected Messages*, book 1, 202)
>
> The enemy of our souls is earnestly at work to introduce among the Lord's people pleasing speculation, and incorrect views regarding the personality [personhood] of God. …
>
> I have seen the results of these fanciful views of God, in apostasy, spiritualism, freelovism. The free love tendencies of these teachings were so concealed that it was difficult to present them in their real character. …
>
> There is a strain of spiritualism coming in among our people, and it will undermine the faith of those who give place to it, leading them to give heed to seducing spirits, and doctrines of devils. (*Manuscript Releases*, vol. 8, 607)
>
> What kind of spiritualism is it that will fool us?
>
> Never allow yourself to be drawn into discussion regarding the personality of God. On this subject, silence is eloquence. (*Manuscript Releases*, vol. 11, 318)
>
> What about the alpha—Kellogg's mystical deception?
>
> We need not the mysticism that is in this book. Those who entertain these sophistries will soon find themselves in a position where the enemy can talk with them, and lead them away from God. (*Selected Messages*, book 1, 202)

> The omega will follow, and will be received by those who are not willing to heed the warning God has given. (Ibid., 200)

These statements all contain truths that every Seventh-day Adventist needs to understand. The "personality" of God that Ellen White referred to does not mean His character, as we use the word today, but referred to His "personhood," or nature. We are told "silence is eloquence," concerning this subject. We are also counseled against believing that we can know where His presence is located. Think about what it means to enter into the "silence" and going into the presence of God. Who do we think we are if we believe we can call upon God to come into our personal presence whenever we want to?

Knowing these things, what is the only hope for God's people to be safe? Isn't it the same hope that Martin Luther, the great father of the Protestant Reformation, had—to trust in the inspiration of God and to distrust pantheistic mysticism? This was the deception that led his contemporary, Ignatius Loyola, the founder of modern spiritual formation, astray. This is the deception that leads many astray today, those who have decided to return to the teachings of Babylon and the emerging church. The teachings of The One Project have absorbed those of the emerging church and include spiritual formation, constructed upon Loyola's spiritual exercises.

Luther learned to have simple faith in the promises he found in the Holy Bible. He studied the Scriptures like a babe, accepting all as if the God of heaven were standing before him, speaking to him personally. Fundamentally speaking, he discovered that the Holy Bible is the unerring Word of God and is the standard of faith and doctrine for every true Christian, containing all the instruction needed for our salvation. He trusted in and relied on the inspiration of the Holy Spirit, which we as Seventh-day Adventists have personally through the Spirit of Prophecy.

As I shared in *The Omega Rebellion*, we know about the history of spiritual formation and how this discipline was built upon the satanically inspired revelations of Ignatius Loyola, founder of what Ellen White called one of the cruelest organizations that ever existed, the Jesuits. These teachings, which are central to the discipline of spiritual formation, are in a book with the title *The Spiritual Exercises of Ignatius Loyola*. This book is required reading, along with a host of other books written by the leaders of the emerging church movement as well as by many Roman Catholic mystics and spiritualists. These are the teachings that people chose to study when they attended George Fox University, falsely believing that they could separate truth from error. Now they have taken their deceptions back to our church members and the youth in our schools. The official mission statement of Vatican II declares spiritual formation to be:

1. A Roman Catholic teaching based on the supernatural revelations of Ignatius Loyola, founder of the Jesuits.

2. That Ignatian spirituality (spiritual formation) is to be the main teaching used to evangelize the world and to win all Christians back to the mother church; back to Roman Catholicism. [11]

These Roman Catholic teachings are what these individuals had to study at George Fox University. Much of what they learned are the beliefs of all those authors, teachers, and pastors as recommended in *The Green Cord Dream*. Four of the others behind the One Project also took courses and had advisors who believed and practiced mysticism. They have studied and espoused the value of spiritual formation.

With this understanding, the frame of reference of the leaders and founders and their positions of influence of our youth, we can move to Roman Catholic theology and its emergent mysticism.

Roman Catholicism

We have said that its theology contains elements of Roman Catholicism. Let's continue to explore this and bring to light appropriate evidence, establishing the progression of events.

Contemplative Outreach: Father Thomas Keating

> Fr. Thomas Keating is a founding member and the spiritual guide of Contemplative Outreach, LTD. He has served on Contemplative Outreach's Board of Trustees since the organization's beginning and is currently serving as the Chairman of the Board. Fr. Keating is one of the principal architects and teachers of the Christian contemplative prayer movement and, in many ways, Contemplative

11 See http://www.vatican.va/archive/hist_councils/ii_vatican_council/documents/vat-ii_decree_19651207_ad-gentes_en.html (accessed February 12, 2014).

Outreach is a manifestation of his longtime desire to contribute to the recovery of the contemplative dimension of Christianity.

Fr. Keating's interest in contemplative prayer began during his freshman year at Yale University in 1940 when he became aware of the Church's history and of the writings of Christian mystics. Prompted by these studies and time spent in prayer and meditation, he experienced a profound realization that, on a spiritual level, Scripture calls people to a personal relationship with God. Fr. Keating took this call to heart. He transferred to Fordham University in New York and, while waiting to be drafted for service in World War II, he received a deferment to enter seminary. Shortly after graduating from an accelerated program at Fordham, Fr. Keating entered an austere monastic community of the Trappist Order in Valley Falls, Rhode Island in January of 1944, at the age of 20. He was ordained a priest in June of 1949.

In March of 1950 the monastery in Valley Falls burned down and, as a result, the community moved to Spencer, Massachusetts. Shortly after the move, Fr. Keating became ill with a lung condition and was put into isolation in the city hospital of Worcester, Massachusetts for nine weeks. After returning to the monastery, he stayed in the infirmary for two years. Fr. Keating was sent to Snowmass, Colorado in April of 1958 to help start a new monastic community called St. Benedict's. He remained in Snowmass until 1961, when he was elected abbot of St. Joseph's in Spencer, prompting his move back to Massachusetts. He served as abbot of St. Joseph's for twenty years until he retired in 1981 and returned to Snowmass, where he still resides today.

During Fr. Keating's term as abbot at St. Joseph's and in response to the reforms of Vatican II, he invited teachers from the East to the monastery. As a result of this exposure to Eastern spiritual traditions, Fr. Keating and several of the monks at St. Joseph's were led to develop the modern form of Christian contemplative prayer called Centering Prayer. Fr. Keating was a central figure in the initiation of the Centering Prayer movement. He offered Centering Prayer workshops and retreats to clergy and laypeople and authored articles and books on the method and fruits of Centering

Prayer. In 1983, he presented a two-week intensive Centering Prayer retreat at the Lama Foundation in San Cristabol, New Mexico, which proved to be a watershed event. Many of the people prominent in the Centering Prayer movement today attended this retreat. Contemplative Outreach was created in 1984 to support the growing spiritual network of Centering Prayer practitioners. Fr. Keating became the community's president in 1985, a position he held until 1999.

Fr. Keating is an internationally renowned theologian and an accomplished author. He has traveled the world to speak with laypeople and communities about contemplative Christian practices and the psychology of the spiritual journey, which is the subject of his *Spiritual Journey* video and DVD series. Since the reforms of Vatican II, Fr. Keating has been a core participant in and supporter of interreligious dialogue. He helped found the Snowmass Interreligious Conference, which had its first meeting in the fall of 1983 and continues to meet each spring. Fr. Keating also is a past president of the Temple of Understanding and of the Monastic Interreligious Dialogue. [12]

Here is the beginning of modern spiritual formation according to the dictates of Vatican II. Father Keating brought the Eastern contemplative methods into the church, even though they were nothing new to the ancient and modern mystics of the church. It was the lay people who needed to be educated in this type of mysticism. He helped to take mysticism to the regular church members of the modern era where spiritual formation continues to be taught throughout the Christian world today. This is the threat to the Seventh-day Adventist Church as our leaders seek to learn these methods from those in the fallen churches.

When the founders of The One Project chose to enroll in George Fox University, they violated the beliefs and standards that we as Seventh-day Adventists have believed for 150 years. They rejected the counsel God gave His remnant church, which can only result in a drifting away from the truth we have held so dear since God called us out of Babylon. This group obviously did not heed the warnings the Lord gave us; warnings meant to protect us and keep us from falling into the very trap that has snared them.

---

12 "Fr. Thomas Keating," Contemplative Outreach, http://www.contemplativeoutreach.org/fr-thomas-keating (accessed February 10, 2014).

Why? Who can read the heart? There could be many reasons, but here are a few possibilities:

> There is still another class who have had great light and special conviction, and a genuine experience in the workings of the Spirit of God; but the manifold temptations of Satan have overcome them. They do not appreciate the light that God has given them. They do not heed the warnings and reproofs from the Spirit of God. They are under condemnation. These will ever be at variance with the straight testimony because it condemns them. (*Testimonies for the Church*, vol. 3, 361)

The Spirit of Prophecy adds this wise counsel:

> How vain is the help of man when Satan's power is exercised over a human being who has become self-exalted and who knows not that he is partaking of the science of Satan. In his self-confidence he walks right into the enemy's trap and is ensnared. He did not heed the warnings given and was taken as Satan's prey. If he had walked humbly with God, he would have run into the trysting place God had provided for him. Thus in times of danger he would have been safe, for God would have lifted for him a standard against the enemy. (*Mind, Character, and Personality*, vol. 2, 725, 726)

The special instructions God gave to us contain warnings against listening to the preaching and teaching of those who mix truth and error. We're told that it is not safe to attend their meetings, so we can easily see the rebellion in choosing to be educated in their schools. We repeat the following statement because it needs to be repeated:

> God is displeased with us when we go to listen to error, without being obliged to go; for unless He sends us to those meetings where error is forced home to the people by the power of the will, He will not keep us. The angels cease their watchful care over us, and we are left to the buffetings of the enemy, to be darkened and weakened by him and the power of his evil angels; and the light around us becomes contaminated with the darkness. (*Early Writings*, 124)

This statement is filled with God's warnings and the consequences of its rejection. In case some would point to her words that say, "for unless He sends us to those meetings" as a reason for their actions, it should be understood that it would never be acceptable to attend the schools of Babylon to receive their education with the intent to bring back theology that conflicts with that of Seventh-day Adventism to young students, giving rise to an opposing movement. Since it has become so common for our pastors and others to attend these schools, it is excusable for one to think that it can be acceptable. If one is led there to study, analyze, and do certain research as a part of their education (excluding searching for light and truth or how to perform our mission) and they are sure God has shown them that this is His will, fine. What makes the case under study unacceptable is their choice of courses and their joining with the emerging church movement—a movement with spiritualist mentors and leaders. Additionally, what would be the reason an Adventist pastor would get their doctor of ministry degree in leadership and emerging culture? This is a course of study which we as Adventists should fear, knowing it has originated from the Roman Catholic Church and involves spiritualism, mystic mentors, and spiritual formation. A doctoral degree is a professional degree, meant to improve one's ability as a pastor, not to prepare for, or learn to do rigorous research. That is the function of a PhD degree. What is so disturbing about their choice is the fact that we offer a doctorate in ministry at our own seminary. Why would a pastor go to a university of Babylon to be a better pastor, a school whose teachers probably never heard of the three angels' messages? And why would they take a course of study in leadership and emerging culture? Either they are totally unaware of the mission of our church, or possibly, they are aware and desire to change it.

Nothing can change the fact that this new movement in our church acts, feels, smells, sings, teaches, and in every way, is like all the other emergent churches, even distributing Dr. Leonard Sweet's teachings. So it is not simply about attending a certain school, it is about joining hands with the emergent culture, then bringing those teachings back to our youth and church members, a seemingly blatant rejection of our inspired counsel. By these actions they have opened themselves to the next stage of deception described once again in the statement repeated below:

> Just as long as men consent to listen to these sophistries, a subtle influence will weave the fine threads of these seductive theories into their minds, and men who should turn away from the first

> sound of such teaching will learn to love it. As loyal subjects we must refuse even to listen to these sophistries. Their influence is something like a deadly viper, poisoning the minds of all who listen. It is a branch of hypnotism, deadening the sensibilities of the soul. (*Manuscript Releases*, vol. 10, 163)

When one listens, having rejected the counsel to not attend these meetings or go to their schools except for the right reasons, the next stage to develop will be the result of being hypnotized, described below:

> I tell you in the name of the Lord God of Israel, that Satan is presenting his sophistries to ministers and medical workers, and if our people listen to these sophistries, they will become impregnated with the same false idea of a popular religion that will cause them to develop into gods, and there will be no place in their lives for God or for Christ. (Ibid.)

Those who refuse God's counsel, and will not heed the warnings God gives will "develop into gods, and there will be no place in their lives for God or for Christ." The fact is that their minds have been taken over with a form of hypnotism. Ellen White said it is a "branch of hypnotism" where the fine threads of satanic thoughts are woven into our minds. I am confident that this is why those involved with these practices resist any counsel. It matters not to them what the Spirit of Prophecy says. This does not mean they will not proclaim Christ, but it will not be the authentic Jesus, for they have rejected His counsel and are in danger of rejecting Him. They then proclaim a false Christ.

> But we are brothers and sisters of all Christians around the world who proclaim Jesus as the Christ. We haven't been given the authority to delegitimize the sonship, daughtership, or siblingship of Christ's followers who differ from us in belief or behavior. Adventists can be true to their John the Baptist calling while sitting at the Thanksgiving table with Christian brothers and sisters. … as Adventist Christians engage the world, we do so viewing others not as the enemy but as beloved siblings. … Are we a separate body

> of Christ, or does Christ have—as Paul says in 1 Corinthians 1 and Ephesians 4—only one body?[13]

According to the above paragraph, anyone who proclaims Jesus as Lord, however He is construed, is a sibling in Christ. This, friends, is Roman Catholicism, not Seventh-day Adventism.

These are the inevitable results of the actions taken by the founders of this project. They have rejected God's counsel, attended the schools of Babylon, had mystics for advisors, and have now come to theological conclusions that agree with Roman Catholicism. This was exactly what the counsel above indicated would take place. They would lose sight of truth and drift into Satan's deception—Roman Catholic teachings.

Now, a brief study of that theology and the elements of Roman Catholicism within it.—The famous Roman Catholic theologian Augustine is quoted in the new Catholic Catechism, and writes:

> 33 The human person: with his openness to truth and beauty, his sense of moral goodness, his freedom and the voice of his conscience, with his longings for the infinite and for happiness, man questions himself about God's existence. In all this he discerns signs of his spiritual soul. The soul, the "seed of eternity we bear in ourselves, irreducible to the merely material," can have its origin only in God.[14]

The Catechism also makes these statements:

> 44 Man is by nature and vocation a religious being. Coming from God, going toward God, man lives a fully human life only if he freely lives by his bond with God.
>
> 47 The Church teaches that the one true God, our Creator and Lord, can be known with certainty from his works, by the natural light of human reason (cf. Vatican Council I, can. 2 § 1: DS 3026).[15]

---

13 Alex Bryan, *The Green Cord Dream. Nampa, ID:* Pacific Press Publishing Association, 2012, 34, 35

14 http://www.vatican.va/archive/ccc_css/archive/catechism/p1s1c1.htm (accessed February 11, 2014)

15 Ibid.

Here are Pope John Paul II's anthropological views. They are telling!

> "Jesus is "the new man" (cf. Eph. 4:24; Col. 3:10), who calls redeemed humanity to share in his divine life. The mystery of the Incarnation lays the foundations for an anthropology which, reaching beyond its own limitations and contradictions, moves toward God himself, indeed toward the goal of "divinization."
>
> This occurs through the grafting of the redeemed on to Christ and their admission into the intimacy of the Trinitarian life. …" [16]

From the theology expressed above we can conclude that Roman Catholicism believes that all people naturally have God's Spirit in them and that we naturally drift toward God, even to the point of the "divinization" of the race, in Christ.

Augustine claims that the person "discerns signs of his spiritual soul"; the soul, the "seed of eternity we bear in ourselves, irreducible to the merely material." This is alluding to the belief in the immortality of the soul, but even more to the belief that the soul naturally discerns its spirituality and thus naturally seeks God. This we know is error and that the fallen soul does not seek God. God comes seeking us; without God seeking us, we would never even have a spiritual thought but would do evil continually:

> The natural, selfish mind, if left to follow out its own evil desires, will act without high motives, without reference to the glory of God or the benefit of mankind. The thoughts will be evil, and only evil, continually. The soul can be in a state of peace only by relying upon God, and by partaking of the divine nature through faith in the Son of God. The Spirit of God produces a new life in the soul, bringing the thoughts and desires into obedience to the will of Christ, and the inward man is renewed in the image of Him who works in us to subdue all things unto himself. (*The Review and Herald*, June 12, 1888)

Jesus told us that when He returns, things on earth would be as they were, "in the days of Noah." What does Scripture say about those days? "God saw that the wickedness of man was great in the earth, and that

16 Howard, *The Omega Rebellion*, 189

every imagination of the thoughts of his heart was only evil continually" (Genesis 6:5).

The belief that every person claiming Jesus as Lord is a brother or sister in the Lord goes against what we know to be truth. Once again it is inspiration in Scripture and in the Spirit of Prophecy that saves the day and explains the truth concerning these things:

> In *Living Temple* the assertion is made that God is in the flower, in the leaf, in the sinner. But God does not live in the sinner. The Word declares that He abides only in the hearts of those who love Him and do righteousness. God does not abide in the heart of the sinner; it is the enemy who abides there." (*Sermons and Talks*, vol. 1, 343)

Jesus dwells only in the hearts of those who love Him, and seek after righteousness—the keeping of the divine law. It is Satan who dwells in the hearts of all others. "Whatever may be the ecstasies of religious feeling, Jesus cannot abide in the heart that disregards the divine law. God will honor those only who honor Him" (*The Sanctified Life*, 92).

This is "why and how" the fallen churches have become the daughters of Babylon—they have rejected the first and second angels' messages delivered to them in the summer of 1844, and subsequently the law of God. This is why in general, according to Inspiration, the members of these churches do not have Jesus living in their hearts and are not our brothers and sisters in the Lord. We have always considered the fallen churches to be Babylon's daughters, and believed that Satan rules their churches and their lives. There are many true Christians who are living up to the light they have within these churches. This is why God has called us to give the loud cry for God's true people dwelling within these churches to come out of them into the Lord's remnant church.

Please understand that it is our love for these people that motivates us to evangelize and dedicate our lives for their salvation. We should be willing to sacrifice—even unto death—so they might have life. But until anyone accepts the Lord as Savior and strives to follow Him and His righteousness, keeping the law according to the light they have, they are not our siblings, or brothers and sisters in the Lord. This false belief is leaven to the three angels' messages, for if we consider all members of these churches as our Christian brothers and sisters, for what purpose should they leave their churches? To consider them such does not agree with the claims of the Spirit of Prophecy.

> As the churches refused to receive the first angel's message, they rejected the light from heaven and *fell from the favor of God.* (*EW* 237.2)

There would be no reason for them to leave and we would have no reason to repeat the loud cry of the second angel, calling them to come out. It is true that there are many true Christians in all the fallen churches, waiting to hear God's call to come out of her my people, but this truth does not mean we should consider every member of all the fallen churches to be our brothers and sisters in the Lord.

Let's see if we can understand the dynamics of what has taken place. First there was deception, then the influence of the false teaching. First there was the enticement of the provocative practices of Egypt (Babylon), then the perverted understanding of truth, as the Israelites of old (Isaiah, chapter 30). The theology of Augustine is found heavier in the balance because of his choosing the teachings and tutelage of mystics instead of the Bible and the Spirit of Prophecy.

Can you now see that to accept everyone in these churches as brothers and sisters when they have en masse rejected the law of God and belong to churches we consider Babylon's daughters is dangerous and especially destructive to our mission to call people out of Babylon?

The acceptance as siblings of all who claim Jesus as their Lord slides right into Roman Catholicism's understanding that all people are on a journey back to God as a result of their spiritual souls' leading. Also, this belief happens to be the very same pantheism held by Dr. John Harvey Kellogg, explained in his infamous book, *Living Temple.*

The Spirit of Prophecy warned us that deceptions based on these very teachings would threaten the church near the close of probation. This is why, as God's people, we must heed the warnings He has given. We cannot be aware of every deception brought before the church, but we can understand the principles God has revealed that point to the dangers. Pantheistic theology, one of those danger signals, is an underlying teaching of The One Project. Its theology is very much out of touch with the inspired teaching that Jesus only dwells in the hearts of "those who love Him and do righteousness," and that "God does not abide in the heart of the sinner; it is the enemy who abides there." (*Sermons and Talks*, vol. 1, 343).

Is condemnation of and frequent warring against God's remnant church, even labeling it a cult, in keeping with the Bible's brotherhood of Christ?

Before we examine the theology of *The Green Cord Dream*, consider these thoughts from the Biblical Research Institute about certain teachings in this book. The following is from their review and is in response to what is found on page 43. The author suggests that we have too many "fistfights" over troublesome passages, usually passages of "lesser questions," matters that he says the Bible leaves "opaque." The Biblical Research Institute then speaks to his use of the term "Babylon," or rather his wrong use of it. This is most interesting since his misapplication of the term reveals how and why he and his colleagues believe that it is acceptable to attend the schools of Babylon. It is acceptable to them because there remains a question of whether or not they believe the fallen churches comprise Babylon. Let's consider what the BRI found.

> With the author this reviewer deplores the theological controversies in the church, but in contrast to him this reviewer does not believe that these controversies concern matters that the Bible leaves opaque (p. 43).
>
> Creation, salvation, the remnant, the sanctuary, and the Spirit of Prophecy, are not opaque matters in Scripture. To give this impression to the young people is doing them a disservice. It will only further alienate them from studying these doctrines for themselves.
>
> Like most critics, the author (p. 47) loves Ellen White's statement that "There is no excuse for anyone in taking the position that there is no more truth to be revealed" (*Counsels to Writers and Editors*, 35), but let's not forget that she also said, "Many of our people do not realize how firmly the foundation of our faith has been laid" (*Selected Messages*, book 1, 206). We have made a few adjustments in our doctrines since the days of our pioneers. They did not teach the doctrine of the trinity, or that the investigative judgment in Daniel 7 also concerns the little horn. Further Bible study has made these things clear. However, we do not change our doctrines merely to accommodate modern trends or opinions, like evolution or a homosexual lifestyle.
>
> A typical case of accommodation to modern trends in theology, even in some Seventh-day Adventist circles, is the author's statement that Babylon is "representative of all totalitarian regimes

> throughout history" (p. 71). Most totalitarian regimes in history were political regimes; the little horn of Daniel and the Babylon of the book of Revelation is a religious power, and the religious power that fits the prophetic picture is the religious alliance of the papacy, fallen Protestantism and spiritualism; and our young people should know that too.[17]

Like the Biblical Research Institute, I find that the author's use of the term Babylon in his book reveals a misunderstanding of its definition. He separates the United States into the good and the bad, the dragon and the lamb. The bad has to do partly with our use of force, like at the founding of the nation when innocent Native Americans were slaughtered. The good, the lamb, covers a host of spiritual concepts, such as Adventism's radical opposition to killing and destruction. Where do these assumptions come from?

Murder, yes, but killing, not so fast. Destruction—I plan to be standing inside the walls next to my Savior when He does the destroying. Has he forgotten how God's supernatural forces were involved in the creation of this great nation? How even William Miller was convinced of divine intervention in the Battle of Plattsburg when Miller's forces were far outnumbered and his life was mysteriously preserved? Or how angels of God fought next to soldiers in both the Civil and Revolutionary Wars? This was the work of God, and I fear that he does not understand this.

17 Pfandl, *Reflections.*

Chapter Six:

The One Project

Now that we have studied some of the unique developments to transpire before the Lord's return, perhaps we will be able to see where a movement like The One Project fits in, and the role it might play. What is it? Where did it come from? Who is responsible for its creation? To begin to answer these important questions, I refer to The One Project's website, and a report from the Adventist News Network:

> We are committed to the idea that a Jesus-driven, Jesus-bathed, Jesus-backed, Jesus-led, Jesus-filled, Jesus-powered, all-about-Jesus Adventist Church is the uncompromising directive from our past, the joy of our present, and hope for our future. We claim the Primal Adventist Impulse: a longing to be with Jesus.
>
> We believe pulpits, classrooms, worship halls, board rooms, living rooms—life!—should be drenched in the Spirit of Jesus.
>
> We crave a "High Christology"—where Jesus is fully honored as Creator, Savior, and Lord. We believe Jesus is the hope of the First Testament and inspiration for the Second. Theology—the study of God—is at its best in dedicated exploration of Jesus, who is "the image of God." We are convicted that he alone is The Desire of the Ages. All of them: the prelapsarian age and life after the fall; the antediluvian age and life after the flood; prehistoric times, the stone age, the classical age, the age of antiquity, the middle ages, the age of reason, the modern age and in this, our 21st Century Age.
>
> We love our church. And so we want the greatest gift for it... Jesus.

The One Project seeks—through gatherings, conversations, web-based content, and Christ-focused publications—to stimulate preaching, worship, and adoration of Jesus within and through the Adventist church.[18]

The annual gathering of The One Project has its roots in Japhet De Oliveira's 2009 cancer diagnosis, which he says was a wake-up call.

With the threat of a worsening sickness looming over him, De Oliveira met with a support group for two days in a Denver hotel in 2010. He and four fellow pastors revealed and examined issues in their lives. Now, his cancer in remission, De Oliveira has seen that small group grow into an annual gathering of hundreds of Seventh-day Adventists seeking to reconnect with Jesus in their personal and corporate worship.

This year's gathering of The One Project on February 13 and 14 brought more than 700 people to Seattle for conversations on practical applications of Jesus' ministry in their own lives, churches and communities. De Oliveira hopes it's an environment where people can honestly look at their own priorities, examine the core of Christianity, and promote Jesus in their theology as Seventh-day Adventists.

For some, it's a place to challenge and even question one's own beliefs.

"We're trying to create a safe place to say Jesus is the center of our church and always has been," said De Oliveira, chaplain for missions at Andrews University in Berrien Springs, Michigan. He's especially looking to support those who may become frustrated with the church.

"We love our church. I really do believe that God has called the Seventh-day Adventist Church and I'm tired of losing people when we work so hard to bring them in," he said.
The One Project is short on programming and long on discussions. De Oliveira says the event format grew out of his wish to make a

18 "Why," The One Project. https://the1project.org/why.html (accessed January 23, 2014)

gathering similar to the best part of the numerous conferences he attends each year—talking with people individually. A small stage is set in the middle of a banquet room and speakers are allowed 20 minutes to present. The event is then geared toward the 40 minutes of discussion at each table following the speaker.

"I go to so many conferences and so many meetings and honestly the best part is meeting with someone over lunch," De Oliveira said. "We didn't want to have another event that's packed with programming all day."

The gathering is also short on exhibitors. The only ones allowed are publishers.

"By reading people will learn and change and transform their lives," De Oliveira said.

Sam Leonor, senior chaplain at La Sierra University, highlighted the 1888 meeting of the Adventist world church body at [the] General Conference Session in Minneapolis, Minnesota, when leaders discussed righteousness by faith. "From that meeting in 1888, Adventists emerged re-focused on Jesus: crucified, living, and coming again," Leonor said.

Dr. David Kim, a family practice physician from Atlanta, said The One Project gathering was long overdue. "I grew up in a legalistic Adventist culture where the three R's dominated—rules, regulations, and rituals. Missing was the biggest R of Christianity—a relationship with Jesus."

The original meeting in Denver in July of 2010 brought the five pastors together for support and soul searching. De Oliveira admits he had "sort of lost [his] way," focusing on success as a pastor and not caring enough for his family or health. "I would only read the Bible to prepare sermons," he said.

The original five were De Oliveira; Leonor; Alex Bryan, pastor of Walla Walla University Church; Tim Gillespie, young adult pastor at Loma Linda Church; and Terry Swenson, senior chaplain at Loma Linda University.

"It was a real honest conversation," De Oliveira said. "Some crying and a lot of praying. We said, 'let's do this at least once a year.'"

The group agreed to meet annually to focus on Jesus. Each invited friends for a similar meeting the following year in Atlanta. More than 170 people showed up.

For that 2011 gathering in Atlanta, participants may not have fully understood what they were coming to, De Oliveira said. They were each asked to read the four gospels and the book *Desire of Ages*, authored by Adventist Church co-founder Ellen G. White. The invitation then was simply, "Come have a two-day conversation about Jesus."[19]

It is not easy to understand how those who claim to love the Seventh-day Adventist Church can accept and practice the teachings meant to win the world to Roman Catholicism, the beast of Revelation chapter 13—the very teachings of which Seventh-day Adventist's have been called to warn the world.

Why would Adventist preachers and teachers proclaim these foreign doctrines that are meant to break down the barriers that separate us from the churches of Babylon if they loved our church?

It seems that they are now believing and teaching Babylon's theology, a result of their choice to ignore counsel in the Spirit of Prophecy, and of choosing Babylon's schools rather than our own. Their actions and choices seem to verify that they do not properly understand the purpose or mission of God's church.

Historically, Seventh-day Adventist thought and mission rests firmly upon the foundation of the three angels' messages. It is the purpose of our existence, and the Spirit of Prophecy states that had we kept this in focus, we would have been in heaven by now. But it seems there are those who want to further distance themselves and our church from this

19 Ansel Oliver, "The One Project Makes Jesus Center of Theology," Adventist New Network, February 17, 2012, http://news.adventist.org/all-news/news/go/2012-02-17/the-one-project-makes-jesus-center-of-theology/ (accessed February 11, 2014).

message, who want to embrace the emergent church model instead. Is this further delaying the Lord's return? Sadly, one can find the evidence of this very problem in the church, where the teachings from emergent church authors are being read and taught from our pulpits. It appears as though The One Project is led by those who no longer feel comfortable in their old neighborhood, and have decided to move away from home. They have lived with God's people under the three angels' messages and the rain of the Spirit, but have now moved under the umbrella of the emerging church, where the rain cannot touch them, and they are shielded from the truth.

There is something the reader needs to be aware of concerning the list of authors recommended in *The Green Cord Dream.* The following list contains every author referred to in the book who is not a Seventh-day Adventist. First the list, then what's interesting:

The List

- Dan Kimball
- David Kinneman
- Jim Palmer
- Andrew Farley
- Lauren Winner
- Deborah A. Wuest
- Walter Wink
- Shane Clairborne
- Tom Peters

Now, the interesting part—every one of these authors practices spiritualism by advocating spiritual formation and the emerging church. Think about this, friends. Every book recommended in *The Green Cord Dream*, aside from those by Seventh-day Adventist authors—every single one was written by someone who believes and teaches spiritual formation—the spiritualism of Roman Catholic and Jesuit emergent theology. Does this not concern you as a Seventh-day Adventist? Even out of the few Adventists quoted, two of them (Bull and Lockhart, 82, GCD), support the teachings of spiritual formation.

At an Adventist forum meeting held at Walla Walla University, on October 11, 2011, Dr. Bryan displayed his favorite spiritual formation books, describing them as "the most helpful." He named the authors—Manning, Foster, Yaconelli, Foster, Willard, Eldredge, Foster, Manning.

These are all emergent teachers and leaders who are also mystics and spiritualists. Please consider the following: Below is a small sample of books and their authors, 11 in all. These were taken from a list of 103 authors recorded in the bibliography of Dr. Bryan's dissertation for his doctoral degree.

Upon examination of every one of those 103 authors, it was discovered that all of them, without exception, are advocates of spiritual formation, writing, teaching and holding seminars on the subject. They are all involved in the changing and new emerging Christianity which supports mystical practices.

It seems there must have been a well thought-out plan to have it that way. What is so interesting though is not the plan, but the fact that it appears to be this way on purpose. It seems that those who believe and teach this discipline were sought after to be the prominent influence in the construction of his dissertation. The consideration of this fact helps us to understand where the changes that are desired might have come from—those who have influenced the writing of his dissertation—Emergent thinkers and philosophers.

Every book studied to prepare his dissertation for the degree in "Leadership and Emerging Culture" was written by someone who is immersed in the theology and mission of the emerging church, and who believes in and practices Roman Catholic spiritual formation. Three others of the original five who founded The One Project, four of the five, earned the same degree in "Leadership and Emerging Culture" from the same school and together, began a movement the same as other emerging church movements.

With this in mind, consider the authors' counsel to have youth take over the church by controlling of all the important boards and committees.

> "*We need pastorates, pulpits, committees, boards, and initiatives filled with very young adults. Not tokens. Not the one 27-year-old who is really a 77-year-old in a 20-something body.* ... Now we must give them the keys to the bakery before we have to put a going-out-of business sign on the window." (*Adventist Today*, Winter 2009, 10, emphasis added)

Remember, by the Roman Catholic Church's own teaching and claims, spiritual formation is a discipline they created and own; it is their baby and is meant to win the entire world back to their spiritual communion.

> "Religious institutes of the contemplative and of the active life, have so far played, and still do play, the main role in the evangelization of the world." (Decree *Ad Gentes* on the Mission Activity of the Church, Vatican II).

Contemplative spirituality and spiritual formation have mystical components that lie at the heart of the end time deception which Seventh-day Adventists have been called to warn the world about. Here, we have pastors and leaders within our church who have gone back to the churches and schools of Babylon to learn these deceptive practices, earning the degrees they offer and have brought them back to God's church disguised in a movement called The One Project.

The Author's Dissertation:

The Role of Human Emotion in Christian Discipleship
a dissertation submitted to the faculty of George Fox Evangelical Seminary
in candidacy for the degree of Doctor of Ministry
by Alex Bryan
Newberg, Oregon, March 2009

Bibliography

Selected emergent and contemplative authors.

Hirsch, Alan. *The Forgotten Ways: Reactivating the Missional Church.* Grand Rapids: Baker Books, 2006.

Kimball, Dan. They Like Jesus but Not the Church: Insights from Emerging Generations. Grand Rapids: Zondervan, 2007.

Kinnamen, David. *Unchristian: What a New Generation Really Thinks About Christianity...and Why It Matters*. Grand Rapids: Baker Books, 2007.

Manning, Brennan. *Abba's Child: The Cry of the Heart for Intimate Belonging.* Colorado Springs: Nav Press, 2002.

Nouwen, Henri J. M. *Here and Now: Living in the Spirit.* New York: The Crossroad Publishing Company, 1994.

Ortberg, John. *The Life You've Always Wanted: Spiritual Disciplines for Ordinary People.*

Peterson, Eugene H. *The Message: The Bible in Contemporary Language.* Grand Rapids: Zondervan, 2002.

___________. *Christ Plays in Ten Thousand Places: A Conversation in Spiritual Theology.* Grand Rapids: Wm. B. Eerdmans Publishing Co., 2005.

___________. *The Jesus Way: A Conversation in the Ways Jesus is the Way.* Grand Rapids: Wm B. Eerdmans Publishing Co., 2007.

Rohr, Richard. *Everything Belongs: The Gift of Contemplative Prayer.* New York: The Crossroad Publishing Company, 2003.

___________. *The Enneagram: A Christian Perspective.* New York: The Crossroad Publishing Company, 2001.

Sweet, Leonard I. *Summoned to Lead.* Grand Rapids: Zondervan, 2004.

___________. *The Gospel According to Starbucks: Living with a Grande Passion.* WaterBrook Press, 2007.

___________. *11: Indispensible Relationships You Can't Be Without.* Colorado Springs: David C. Cook, 2008.

Willard, Dallas. *The Spirit of the Disciplines: Understanding How God Changes Lives.*

__________. *The Divine Conspiracy: Rediscovering Our Hidden Life with God.* New York: Harper Collins Publishers, 1990.

__________. *Renovation of the Heart: Putting on the Character of Christ.* Colorado Springs: Nav Press, 2002.

__________. *The Great Omission: Reclaiming Jesus's Essential Teachings on Discipleship.* HarperSanFrancisco, 2006.

Wright, N.T. *Jesus and the Victory of God.* Minneapolis: Fortress Press, 1996.

__________. *The Challenge of Jesus.* Downers Grove: InterVarsity Press, 1999.

When deciding whether this movement is making our church a safe place to find Jesus, please take into consideration what you have just learned—that four of the five leaders and founders of The One Project have earned their degrees in "Leadership and Emerging Culture" and recommend reading books written by spiritualists and mystics who are members of the churches we believe are the daughters of Babylon. In the following chapters we will continue to investigate the influence that the emerging church has had on the leaders of The One Project.

You may recall that our General Conference president, Ted Wilson, counseled the church at large in his first sermon to God's Church after being selected as president of the General Conference, to be sure not to go outside the church to seek instruction in spiritual formation, and to not invite non-Seventh-day Adventist speakers from the emerging church to speak at our churches. Elder Wilson wisely counsels us, according to the Spirit of Prophecy, to seek our own people to instruct us, people who understand our origins, understand the three angels' messages, the Sabbath, the state of the dead, the soon second coming, etc. That is the qualification for people to instruct us—those who know the biblical truth, and not those who know only a mixture of truth and error. This is the contrast that is important!

In the light of this counsel, we repeat once again that four of the five founders of The One Project received their doctor of ministry in leadership and emerging culture from George Fox University and were all mentored by the university's official mentor for their course of study, Dr. Leonard Sweet, a believer in Christian mysticism and spiritual formation.

Please consider carefully this unusual coincidence. These five founders of The One Project are all employed in positions associated with major colleges and universities, four of them Seventh-day Adventist. Four of them have their doctoral degrees in courses of study that we know are a threat to our spiritual lives, from a university we know we should avoid unless led there by God, something He would never do for a course of study with mystic mentors. One of the five who did not earn a degree in Leadership and Emerging Culture is a chaplain at Andrews University. They continually train our youth in the emerging church theology that they themselves have adopted. It seems that a change in our church is desired by those educated in the schools of Babylon. The fact that these leaders all have a tremendous influence over our youth because of the positions they hold, along with the continual train of speakers invited from outside the church who are spiritualists, is extremely troubling to those of us who are following the progress of this movement in God's church.

Surely all this is something that would have caused Ellen White to say that she "trembled." (*1 Selected Messages*, 204) The type of error found in the teachings of The One Project, is that which the Lord said He would allow to bring about the "shaking."

> God's Spirit has illuminated every page of Holy Writ, but there are those upon whom it makes little impression, because it is imperfectly understood. *When the shaking comes, by the introduction of false theories,* these surface readers, anchored nowhere, are like shifting sand. They slide into any position to suit the tenor of their feelings of bitterness. … *Daniel and Revelation must be studied, as well as the other prophecies of the Old and New Testaments.* Let there be light, yes, light, in your dwellings. For this we need to pray. The Holy Spirit, shining upon the sacred page, will open our understanding, that we may know what is truth. (*Testimonies to Ministers and Gospel Workers*, 112, emphasis added)

Notice how this statement stresses the importance of the study of prophecy in Daniel and the Revelation, the study of which is downplayed by proponents of the emerging church. Many in our church who are involved in this movement agree with this philosophy of downplaying any teachings that would separate the churches from each other. Our unique understanding of the prophecies in the book of Daniel do certainly separate us from the other churches—as they should—and what we might be missing is that those teachings also protect us by keeping us separate.

In 2009, Dr. Bryan, author of *The Green Cord Dream*, wrote an article for the liberal magazine *Adventist Today*. This magazine is known for its articles that appeal to those who are unhappy with the traditional and historical Seventh-day Adventist Church. Here are a few excerpts from his article:

> Or are we simply going to continue to instruct students in desk-and-chalkboard or pulpit-and-pew environments about *the "28" and Adventist Heritage?* … I believe a major paradigm jolt is in order for a church that is *scrambling to find safety* as the tectonic plates of culture quake beneath us. …We need 18- to 22-year-olds trained so that *23- to 35-year-olds can start leading the church. Right away. Then. Now.* … We need holy and hungry, spiritual and sassy,

> Christ-centered and creative young people. … A "piece of the pie" was okay in 1990. But times have changed, for the worse.…
>
> We need pastorates, pulpits, committees, boards, and initiatives filled with very young adults. Not tokens. Not the one 27-year-old who is really a 77-year-old in a 20-something body. … *Now we must give them the keys to the bakery before we have to put a going-out-of business sign on the window.* (*Adventist Today*, Winter 2009, 10, emphasis added)

He says we need "sassy" young people, for whom a "piece of the pie" was okay twenty years ago, to now take over the church to save it—before it goes out of business? I am unaware of any inspired teaching in the Spirit of Prophecy that hints of the church "going out of business."

Another troubling thought has to do with how their message is most attractive to the youth. Successful change is often the result of first influencing the educational institutions of the organization where change is desired. Educate the young people and convince them of your ideas, then move them into positions of authority to bring about the change you desire. In *The Great Controversy*, Ellen White tells us that this strategy was used throughout the centuries by the Jesuits to regain control of the nations who originally converted to Protestantism.

Isn't it interesting that the author of *The Green Cord Dream* expresses that same strategy in the article he wrote for *Adventist Today*? Isn't it also interesting that the theology of The One Project is taken from Jesuit and Roman Catholic theology? Isn't it interesting that all five of the original founders of *The One Project* are employed by the church at our educational institutions? And isn't it interesting that when the radical emergent church leader, Shane Clairborne (see picture below), was invited by Walla Walla University, Clairborne's staff admitted that it was their goal to "to recruit WWU students to join them in the work of their ministry"? And finally, isn't it interesting that Dr. Bryan, the author of the revolutionary book *The Green Cord Dream*, wants young and sassy men and women to move into positions of power and authority within the church?

Many young people desire to be associated with something "new," often driven by the longing to express their individuality, while searching for meaning in their lives. When expressing that individuality on a mission to incorporate whatever these "new" beliefs may be, it is natural to try to remove, or avoid, anything standing in the way—in this case, doctrines.

Doctrines divide and separate. The fundamental teachings of the Seventh-day Adventist Church definitely separate us from all other denominations, and negatively affect any plan that might want to bring changes to the church, which might be behind the author's plan to have young people move into leadership board positions. Without church standards, all the other emergent churches will find it acceptable to befriend Adventists. This is Jesuit teaching and philosophy at its best.

Please consider this: It may be that we have not lost influence with the young people in our church because there is something wrong with our mission, or beliefs, as is suggested by the plans and actions of those behind The One Project. Whatever we have lost may be due to the fact that Satan has successfully introduced the leaven of the world into the church. To keep our young people, The One Project is suggesting that we change our standards and keep the worldly leaven. Moreover, to change the church standards, it is being suggested that we place those searching young people into positions of power and authority. Wouldn't this result in God's church becoming like all the other emerging churches?

Supporters of this program believe this to be the way to win others and bring revival and reformation.

> The enemy of souls has sought to bring in the supposition that a great reformation was to take place among Seventh-day Adventists, and that this reformation would consist in giving up the doctrines which stand as the pillars of our faith, and engaging in a process of reorganization. Were this reformation to take place, what would result? The principles of truth that God in His wisdom has given to the remnant church would be discarded. Our religion would be changed. The fundamental principles that have sustained the work for the last fifty years would be accounted as error. A new organization would be established. Books of a new order would be written. A system of intellectual philosophy would be introduced. The founders of this system would go into the cities, and do a wonderful work. The Sabbath of course, would be lightly regarded, as also the God who created it. Nothing would be allowed to stand in the way of the new movement. The leaders would teach that virtue is better than vice, but God being removed, they would place their dependence on human power, which, without God, is worthless. Their foundation would be built on the sand, and storm and

> tempest would sweep away the structure." *Selected Messages*, book 1, 204, 205).

Notice how many of the points in this prophecy are fulfilled by this movement. Ellen White saw a great reformation, which involved giving up the doctrines, reorganizing, and discarding principles of truth. Principles that sustained the work would be counted as error; new organization, books of a new order, a system of intellectual philosophy introduced. Founders would go into the cities and do a wonderful work. God and the Sabbath would be lightly regarded, and finally, nothing would be able to stand in its way. My friends, I cannot help but tremble as Ellen White did when she beheld the "omega" deception. I'm not claiming this is the omega, but I admit to tremendous concern that this movement will have a degree of success in deceiving faithful Seventh-day Adventists. The Biblical Research Institute shares this concern. When reviewing *The Green Cord Dream*, they wrote that "young and impressionable Adventists will come away from this book with a skewed picture of what Adventism is all about."(BRI Newsletter #42, p. 10, April 2013)

It is worth repeating that the words quoted from the article in *Adventist Today* saying that we need "sassy" young people for whom a "piece of the pie" was okay twenty years ago, does not appear to come from someone who believes with all his heart that we are God's final remnant church that will not fall. Neither do they appear to come from any plan that can be found in the Spirit of Prophecy.

Faithful Seventh-day Adventists would not fear that we would ever have to put a "going out of business sign" in our window. The Lord has promised to see the church through to the end and even if it appears it is about to fall, "it will not fall" (*Selected Messages*, book 2, 380).

> The church may appear as about to fall, but *it does not fall.* It remains, *while the sinners in Zion will be sifted out—the chaff separated from the precious wheat.* This is a terrible ordeal, but nevertheless it must take place. (Ibid., emphasis added)

> As the storm approaches, *a large class who have professed faith in the third angel's message, but have not been sanctified through obedience to the truth, abandon their position and join the ranks of the opposition. (The Great Controversy*, 608, emphasis added)

It seems that the teachers of The One Project may lack a proper understanding of what is in store for God's church or for the people of the world, and are teaching things that the Spirit of Prophecy has warned the church to beware of.

> The words of the prophet declare the solemn responsibility of those who are appointed as guardians of the church of God, stewards of the mysteries of God. They are to stand as watchmen on the walls of Zion, to sound the note of alarm at the approach of the enemy. (*The Acts of the Apostles*, 361)

What they have done, and continue to do as they teach and minister, is in direct defiance of counsel from the Spirit of Prophecy and from our General Conference president. Their actions are in part fulfilling the prophecies concerning the deceptions the church will face shortly before the close of probation.

Considering Inspiration again, the issues involve those that may determine our salvation. How can we possibly give the three angels' messages (part of which is the "loud cry" calling God's people to come out from these churches) when we ourselves choose to attend and earn our advanced degrees at the schools and universities of which we are supposed to warn the world? Once again:

> *God is displeased with us when we go to listen to error, without being obliged to go;* for unless He sends us to those meetings where error is forced home to the people by the power of the will, He will not keep us. *The angels cease their watchful care over us, and we are left to the buffetings of the enemy, to be darkened and weakened by him and the power of his evil angels; and the light around us becomes contaminated with the darkness.*" (*Early Writings*, 125, emphasis added)

Chapter Seven:
The Green Cord Dream

It didn't happen on that day. He didn't appear. The clock struck midnight, and the Adventists were wrong. Tragically wrong. A whopper of a theological mistake. We argued from the Bible that the second coming of Jesus would happen on *this* date. We quit our jobs, left our homes, walked out of our churches. We sold our stuff. We looked to the sky. But there was no trumpet. There were no angels. There was no cloud.

The Advent movement was born in failure rather than success, error rather than truth, darkness rather than light, and sorrow rather than joy. Jesus didn't return.

The Great Disappointment.[20]

Dr. Bryan states that the Adventist movement was born in failure, error, and darkness. This reasoning is troubling. He uses "we" repeatedly, definitely referring to Seventh-day Adventists, revealing a serious and flawed understanding of our history. He is attributing the mistake in time setting to early Seventh-day Adventists. This is not true. It was not early Seventh-day Adventists, but early Millerite Adventists, who made the mistake. Yes, they were called Adventists, but they were not Seventh-day Adventists. God called those who came out of that movement to be His remnant Seventh-day Adventist Church to correct the many errors that existed in the Millerite movement and in the Protestant churches in general after the Great Disappointment. Since He was calling them to be His remnant church, He also called them to search the Scriptures for all the light needed for a proper understanding of its teachings, to shine as His

20 Bryan, *The Green Cord Dream*, 11, 12.

representatives in the world. Consider the following quote from the Spirit of Prophecy:

> The world looked upon our hope as a delusion, and our disappointment as its consequent failure; but though we were mistaken in the event that was to occur at that period, there was *no failure* in reality of the vision that seemed to tarry. (*Life Sketches*, 62, emphasis added)

Not only was there no failure, but there was also no darkness. All was light as God led during every moment of their disappointment, and so the movement was in God's constant control. Ellen White also states that:

> As a people, we should be earnest students of prophecy; we should not rest until we become intelligent in regard to the subject of the sanctuary, which is brought out in the visions of Daniel and John. This subject sheds great light on our present position and work, *and gives us unmistakable proof that God has led us in our past experience. It explains our disappointment in 1844.* (*Evangelism*, 222, 223, emphasis added).

Let's read again:

> "It didn't happen on that day. He didn't appear. The clock struck midnight …
>
> The Advent movement was born in failure rather than success, error rather than truth, darkness rather than light, and *sorrow rather than joy*. Jesus didn't return. (*The Great Disappointment.*[21])

Dr, Bryan defines what he believes is the meaning of this darkness. He says, "The absence of God means total darkness. Evil's ultimate aim."[22] These are his words. He writes that those who experienced the Great Disappointment were in "darkness rather than light." He is thus claiming that it was not God who was in control, but evil. By claiming that the mistake was made because of the absence of God, he is implying the presence of Satan and his deceptions. This is wrong; but more importantly,

21 Ibid., emphasis added.

22 Ibid., *87.*

it is dangerous. In the BRI's review, it was stated by the reviewer that the book left a "skewed picture" of our church.[23] I pray that you are seeing why the reviewer was concerned. The fact is that in the Millerite movement, including in their mistakes, God was at the helm, not Satan. The Lord was fulfilling His purposes. The author reveals how it is his misunderstanding of these things that allows him to be comfortable referring to the Adventist Church, as just "a church."[24]

As we pointed out, it was not our early Seventh-day Adventist Church that was wrong, but the group from which they came. If he had consulted the biblical books of Daniel and Revelation, as Ellen White counseled, he would have seen that which "sheds great light on our present position and work, and gives us unmistakable proof that God has led us in our past experience. It explains our disappointment in 1844" (*Evangelism*, 223). Had he done this, he might not have referred to Millerites as early Seventh-day Adventists, or to the work and leading of the Holy Spirit as "failure," "error," and "darkness."

Inspiration says:

> I saw the people of God joyful in expectation, looking for their Lord. But God designed to prove them. His hand covered a mistake in the reckoning of the prophetic periods. Those who were looking for their Lord did not discover this mistake, and the most learned men who opposed the time also failed to see it. God designed that His people should meet with a disappointment. (*Early Writings*, 235)

Whose hand covered a "mistake in the reckoning of prophetic time"? God's hand! The Lord is "who" caused all these things to occur, not Satan. There was no "darkness" in the mistake made, and what is so disconcerting about the author's assumption that there was, is that he attributes the working of God (the mistake) to a satanic victory (darkness rather than light), with Satan gaining the advantage over, and deceiving, God's people. This is not what occurred. Someone is "tragically wrong," and it is not the Seventh-day Adventists, but the author. Ellen White said there was "no failure," and that God withheld the light according to His will. In light of all this, do you see the danger of casting such a pessimistic shadow over our early history? Such an account gives the young people in our church a false

---

23 Pfandl, *Reflections.*

24 Bryan, "The End of American Adventism?", 10.

understanding of our history—young people who are already in the midst of an identity crisis. Concerning this period of time, Inspiration claims:

> This soul-purifying work led the affections away from worldly things to a consecration never before experienced. ... Thousands were led to embrace the truth preached by William Miller, and servants of God were raised up in the spirit and power of Elijah to proclaim the message. (*Early Writings*, 232, 233)

Let's continue to review the true history of that time using Inspiration:

> This was the happiest year of my life. My heart was full of glad expectation; but I felt great pity and anxiety for those who were in discouragement and had no hope in Jesus. We united, as a people, in earnest prayer for a true experience and the unmistakable evidence of our acceptance with God. (*Life Sketches*, 59)

There was nothing tragic about it. God was behind it all, working out His purposes. No one was "tragically wrong," as he so confusingly states, besides him. Sadly, it seems that he is out of touch with the truth of what occurred, failing to realize how God led our movements at that time, allowing the error, and purposefully preventing His people from seeing the truth. History has been misapplied, facts mixed up, and names, titles, and times confused. The reader is left with false impressions of how God raised up His last-day remnant church. Dr. Bryan's portrayal of our history places him in the camp of others who are at times ashamed of the events surrounding the beginning of our church and who wish they never had to defend our beginnings. These feelings likely originate from a misunderstanding of how God was actually carrying out His purposes and fulfilling His will, leading our founders' every move.

Many disparage God's church because they do not understand God's ways. They wind up blaming perceived error on satanic influences, as we have shown, and have trouble explaining how God could work this way. This confusion can cause feelings of shame and embarrassment, and even resentment toward the church for its failures, all perceived within the book.

When we don't properly understand how the Lord called His remnant church out of the world, resulting in a twisted and darkened account of our history, faithful Seventh-day Adventists need to take heed. The lack of accuracy helps to explain why there is acceptance of certain elements of

Roman Catholicism, leading to the need to bring change to the church—even if by false revival.

During the Great Awakening in the early 1800s, the Lord was preparing to call His people from the fallen churches into the advent movement through the unique message preached by William Miller and others who were convinced of its validity. It was God's plan to bring the attention of the entire world to the second coming of Jesus Christ. To do this, the Lord blocked from their minds the proper interpretation of Daniel 8:14, which in reality was in reference to the cleansing of the sanctuary in heaven. They became convinced that the text was in reference to the timing of Christ's return to this world (the second coming), and that it would occur on October 22, 1844. With this belief, they passionately went about warning the entire world of the Lord's return, eventually reaching every missionary outpost on earth with the message.

This was God's plan and it was carried out by the direct intervention of the Holy Spirit preventing them from having a proper understanding of the verses in question. They believed exactly what God planned for and allowed them to believe. With this understanding, would you call their experience, "darkness rather than light," or "failure rather than success"?

Consider this very carefully, because if we agree with this interpretation of things, we are calling God's will and actions "darkness" and "failure," and are actually blaming this so-called "failure" and "darkness" on the Holy Spirit—something surely no one wants to do. We need to tread carefully, especially when our motives may be to further a cause whose teachings are in disagreement with the mission and teachings of the Seventh-day Adventist Church, God's remnant church and denominated people.

Dr. Bryan expresses doubt that the Seventh-day Adventist Church will be able to fulfill the mission to which God has called it unless it accepts the many radical and revolutionary reforms he and the leaders of The One Project suggest. We previously mentioned an article he wrote a few years ago for *Adventist Today*. In this article we can catch a glimpse of his views. The problem presented is that his suggested reforms disagree with how Inspiration describes the mission and beliefs of God's church. These are the issues in the book, *The Green Cord Dream,* which we will address.

What has been written in this book reveals serious misconceptions of how God works through His people. When these kinds of errors are made because of a refusal to seek God's special instruction in the Spirit of Prophecy, apostasy will always knock at the door. The wrong conclusions in this book were inevitable, the author having chosen the schools of Egypt, setting up an easy prey for Satan's deceptions. Evidence of this is found in the first two chapters, where a misguided understanding of the Great Disappointment is found, as well as in theological concepts that contradict established Seventh-day Adventist beliefs in the remainder of this chapter.

An anemic understanding of our early history is consistently affirmed. To repeat, the Holy Spirit is the One who led throughout, and is the One who intended that those involved would not see the truth. There was no failure, only tremendous success, accomplishing exactly what God wanted to have accomplished. Neither was there any darkness, but rather the purest light, as God's will was being perfectly fulfilled through the work of the Holy Spirit. Darkness is satanic—the absence of light and God's presence.

In His own way, God withheld the truth from the minds of the believers so His purposes could be worked out and prophecy fulfilled. Jesus' triumphal entry into Jerusalem fulfilled Old Testament prophecy from the book of Zechariah. The Lord's entry into Jerusalem upon the foal of an ass to be crowned king is foretold in Zechariah 9:9. The Lord would never have ridden into Jerusalem on that donkey if all involved didn't erroneously believe that He was going to be crowned king. God planned it that way. He led the entire process by withholding light and allowing "mistakes" to be made, as He did in the Great Awakening. In the Great Disappointment, the Lord withheld truth from the believers in order to carry out His plans and fulfill prophecy.

The Lord has consistently withheld truth from His people since the fall in the Garden of Eden. Truth always unfolds slowly, along with the flow of time. God does not always reveal the truth of Scripture just because His people are searching for it, but unfolds it according to His infinite wisdom, as it is needed for that generation. The purpose of doing it this way is so those who are living at that time can accurately recognize where they are in history. This knowledge comes along with an accurate interpretation of prophecy, and most importantly defines their work and calling. The unfolding of the truth in the prophecies of Daniel that were previously sealed until the time of the end, is a perfect example of this principle, defining our duty to prepare the world for the second coming of the Lord.

This is a principle that we need to understand in order to grasp what took place during the Great Disappointment. To not understand how God withholds truth, allowing for "mistakes," as Ellen White called their misunderstanding, results in the belief that satanic forces must be responsible for the "mistakes," tragically permitting the use of words like "darkness," "failure," and "error" to describe the perfect outworking of God's plans.

This is why Ellen White said there was "no failure" and that "God was carrying out His purposes."

Was the Lord's triumphal entry into Jerusalem to be crowned king a failure? Was it error and darkness? These are words that should never be used to describe the working of the Lord. The use of them reveals our own weakness and misunderstanding of how God works.

This is a good time to mention the fact that it is likely the misunderstanding of these very issues that resulted in the founders of The One Project believing it was acceptable to further their education in the schools of Babylon. Instead of recognizing how God was leading us in the beginning of this movement, they attributed the "mistake" to a satanic victory and lost sight of how special our calling out of Babylon was. This is most troubling, as the emergent teachings of the fallen churches are being transferred into the thought processes of our Adventist pastors and youth leaders.

To put it another way, having not comprehended how God called us out from the worldly churches as His peculiar treasure, a unique people whom He separated from the world in order to succeed in the mission He called us to, they found it desirable to return to Egypt to learn how to solve our problems and instruct our youth. And for the excitement found there of hearing something "different," Dr. Bryan has shown by his understanding of the events surrounding the beginnings of our church that he has misapplied history and does not comprehend the working of God properly—how He called us, and how He controlled all that occurred in the movement. He incorrectly attributes the "mistake" to a satanic victory. Correctly understood, the thought of returning to the schools of Egypt and teaching the theology learned there would cause one to shudder in fear. But instead, a kind of resistance to counsel and attempt to prove wrong those who expose the error emerges, a frightening condition from our perspective.

Now, let us return to an accurate record of our history.

Those involved in the great spiritual revival of the first half of the 19th century, culminating in the advent movement, recall those years as being especially blessed by God; a time when they witnessed His wonderful providences, and not generally a time of "sadness." They were disappointed, yes, but there was no failure, error, or darkness, according to the pen of Inspiration. The light of God was with them, even through the disappointment. They were being tested, and all went according to the plan of God.

To misunderstand these wonderful truths is like living within this movement with no heart—having no love for the message, or passion for the very thing God instructs us to remember to give us victory—how He has led us in the past. Because of bad choices, these poor folks don't have an understanding of how God led us in the past, and so, have faltered theologically; they are even embarrassed when they hear the term remnant church, when they should be humbled and exhilarated that God has called them to be a part of the movement. Their refusal to follow inspired counsel has resulted in viewing our movement in the light of the schools they attended—the schools of Egypt and Babylon.

> I saw that God was in the proclamation of the time in 1843. It was His design to arouse the people and bring them to a testing point, where they should decide for or against the truth. Ministers were convinced of the correctness of the positions taken on the prophetic periods, and some renounced their pride, and left their salaries and their churches to go forth from place to place to give the message. But as the message from heaven could find a place in the hearts of but few of the professed ministers of Christ, the work was laid upon many who were not preachers. Some left their fields to sound the message, while others were called from their shops and their merchandise. And even some professional men were compelled to leave their professions to engage in the unpopular work of giving the first angel's message. (*Early Writings*, 232)

Is there found within the description any evidence that the preaching of first angel's message described above was "darkness rather than light, or error rather than truth"? It is called by the Lord's messenger a "message from heaven." Read on to see how ministers laid aside their separate opinions to preach the truth.

> Ministers laid aside their sectarian views and feelings and united in proclaiming the coming of Jesus. Wherever the message was given, it moved the people. Sinners repented, wept, and prayed for forgiveness, and those whose lives had been marked with dishonesty were anxious to make restitution. Parents felt the deepest solicitude for their children. Those who received the message labored with their unconverted friends and relatives, and with their souls bowed with the weight of the solemn message, warned and entreated them to prepare for the coming of the Son of man. Those cases were most hardened that would not yield to such a weight of

evidence set home by heartfelt warnings. This soul-purifying work led the affections away from worldly things to a consecration never before experienced.

Thousands were led to embrace the truth preached by William Miller, and servants of God were raised up in the spirit and power of Elijah to proclaim the message. Like John, the forerunner of Jesus, those who preached this solemn message felt compelled to lay the ax at the root of the tree, and call upon men to bring forth fruits meet for repentance. Their testimony was calculated to arouse and powerfully affect the churches and manifest their real character. And as the solemn warning to flee from the wrath to come was sounded, many who were united with the churches received the healing message; they saw their backslidings, and with bitter tears of repentance and deep agony of soul, humbled themselves before God. And as the Spirit of God rested upon them, they helped to sound the cry, "Fear God, and give glory to Him; for the hour of His judgment is come." (*Early Writings*, 232, 233)

I saw the people of God joyful in expectation, looking for their Lord. But God designed to prove them. *His hand covered a mistake in the reckoning of the prophetic periods.* Those who were looking for their Lord did not discover this mistake, and the most learned men who opposed the time also failed to see it. *God designed that His people should meet with a disappointment.* The time passed, and those who had looked with joyful expectation for their Saviour were sad and disheartened, while those who had not loved the appearing of Jesus, but embraced the message through fear, were pleased that He did not come at the time of expectation. Their profession had not affected the heart and purified the life. The passing of the time was well calculated to reveal such hearts. [The passing of time was well calculated to reveal such hearts—"as in the days of Noah."] They were the first to turn and ridicule the sorrowful, disappointed ones who really loved the appearing of their Saviour. I saw the wisdom of God in proving His people and giving them a searching test to discover those who would shrink and turn back in the hour of trial. (Ibid., 235, 236, emphasis added)
Notice these two major points:

1. Can you see how it was God's hand which hid the truth from His people, His hand covering the mistake, and that it was not a satanic victory of "darkness"?

2. Inspiration calls their experience one which resulted in them being "sad and disheartened," not the almost suicidal, "tragically wrong" portrayed. On the contrary, it was a "healing message" designed to "prove them," and all was according to the "wisdom of God."

In some ways, the record of Adventist history as portrayed in *The Green Cord Dream* is more in keeping with those who mocked the second coming at that time; they were the ones who used the terms "failure and error."

The Theology of *The Green Cord Dream*

The theology taught in *The Green Cord Dream* is revealed in the following quotes, taken from pages 34 and 35. Consider its confusion and disorienting impact. The author wrote:

> If we take Jesus seriously, recognizing that He has jurisdiction and life-or-death power over every human being, then we should see one another as fellow citizens, subjects of the same kingdom. Switching metaphors: if all of us are children of God because He created all of us, then we are … siblings! …
>
> "Are we Christian or cult?" Are we a separate body of Christ, or does Christ have—as Paul says in 1 Corinthians 1 and Ephesians 4—only one body?
>
> Adventism has something particular and important to say to the whole of Christianity—a message unique to us. But we are brothers and sisters of all Christians around the world who proclaim Jesus as the Christ. We haven't been given the authority to delegitimize the sonship, daughtership, or siblingship of Christ-followers who differ from us in belief and behavior. Adventists can be true to their John the Baptist calling while sitting at the Thanksgiving table with Christian brothers and sisters. …

> As Adventist Christians engage the world, we do so viewing others not as the enemy but as beloved siblings whom we hope will come to know God.

Let us first deal with his concept of who he believes are Christians and our siblings. We cannot read hearts, but God has given us light concerning the fallen churches and movements that abound all over the world. They are all fallen, yet are filled with many of God's true children. So the fact that there are sincere Christians everywhere, who know God and are our true siblings and citizens of the "kingdom," is correct, but not all of them are, and there is no way for us to know who they are aside from waiting for the time they will answer the call to "come out of her My people." So they are not all citizens of the kingdom, yet he says, "But we are brothers and sisters of all Christians around the world who proclaim Jesus as the Christ. We haven't been given the authority to delegitimize the sonship, daughtership, or siblingship of Christ's followers who differ from us in belief and behavior." Here, the claim is made that we must consider all those who call Jesus their Lord, brothers and sisters, and we do not have the right to judge them by their beliefs. But then, just a few sentences further he says we should view them, "... not as the enemy but as beloved siblings whom we hope will come to know God."

Dr. Bryan says we should hope that they come to know God, when in the previous sentence concerning this same group, he said we should relate to them as brothers and sisters because they call Jesus Lord. He seems to want things both ways, to not offend anyone. How can we do as he asked, and relate to them all as brothers and sisters, and fellow Christians, if, as he says, they don't know God? Should we make believe—just in case? We should, of course, "treat" everyone as if they were a brother and sister, with the love of Jesus, but the word "consider" is different than "treat," and would mean we must not believe the Spirit of Prophecy when it says:

> *The churches are elated, and consider that God is working marvelously for them, when it is the work of another spirit. The excitement will die away and leave the world and the church in a worse condition* than before. (*Early Writings*, 260, emphasis added)

Notice how this statement says that the people in these churches "consider" that God is working for them when it is Satan. In light of this, how can we then "consider" them brothers and sisters in the Lord?

Another troubling aspect of this movement is how there is cooperation and a merging of worship and other types of celebrating, along with the following of their framework for how the church should function.

We have this statement:

> *"There is to be no compromise with those who make void the law of God. It is not safe to rely upon them as counselors. Our testimony is not to be less decided now than formerly; our real position is not to be cloaked in order to please the world's great men. They may desire us to unite with them and accept their plans, and may make propositions in regard to our course of action which may give the enemy an advantage over us ... You are not to look to the world in order to learn what you shall write and publish or what you shall speak. Let all your words and works testify, We have not followed cunningly devised fables."* [Italics supplied] (2 Peter 1:16 KJV)(2SM 371.1)

Something else to consider is Solomon's example. How can our prayers for them to come to know God through our efforts possibly be fulfilled when those efforts include our disobedience to the counsels God has given us? Those counsels were to not return to the fallen churches to receive new light; to not return to Egypt as Solomon did, satisfying the evil desires of his fallen nature. As Ellen White said concerning Solomon's attempt to win the nations through mingling and taking the kings' daughters in marriage,

> Vain hope! Solomon's mistake in regarding himself as strong enough to resist the influence of heathen associates was fatal. And fatal, too, the deception that led him to hope that notwithstanding a disregard of God's law on his part, others might be led to revere and obey its sacred precepts. ... The king's alliances and commercial relations with heathen nations brought him renown, honor, and the riches of this world. ...but the fine gold of character was dimmed and marred. (*Prophets and Kings*, 54, 55)

The only way to relate to all people, according to his theology, is to treat everyone as fellow Christians. This is very confusing indeed.

Also, if as the author says, we do not have "the authority to delegitimize the sonship, daughtership, or siblingship of Christ-followers who differ from us in belief and behavior," accepting them as brothers and sisters in Christ, does this not conflict with his instruction that we should hope that they "will come to know God"? If we can't judge them and must call them siblings, how can we possibly make an opposite judgment and say that they don't know God? Perhaps individually he is correct, but definitely not corporately, for we know that "Babylon is fallen" (Revelation 18:1–4), and has become filled with evil spirits. It is this truth that defines the mission of the Seventh-day Adventist Church.

I pray that you see the problem in this kind of thinking. We're being told that people who don't know God must be considered family in Christ, totally. The author seems confused concerning what he believes about those in the fallen churches who claim to be Christians. Once again it appears that he is attempting to have things both ways. First we must settle that he is speaking of Christ's kingdom, and not the kingdom of this world. He says:

> Then we should see one another as fellow citizens, subjects of the same kingdom. Switching metaphors: if all of us are children of God because He created all of us, then we are …siblings! …
>
> "Are we Christian or cult?" Are we a separate body of Christ, or does Christ have—as Paul says in 1 Corinthians 1 and Ephesians 4—only one body? [25]

Obviously, he is speaking of Christ's kingdom, which brings us to another problem, pantheism. Pantheism was a part of the deception that swept the church during the Kellogg years, and we have been warned that we will encounter similar theories as we near the close of probation (see Final Remarks at the end of this chapter). His belief that Jesus reigns in every heart because He is our creator hints of pantheistic tendencies. Once again, he is confusing in the expression of his beliefs. In one place he says:

> If we take Jesus seriously, recognizing that He has jurisdiction and life-or-death power over every human being, then we should see one another as fellow citizens, subjects of the same kingdom. Switching metaphors: if all of us are children of God because He created all of us, then we are… siblings! [26]

---

25 Bryan, *The Green Cord Dream,* 34, 35.

26 Ibid., 34.

He claims that we are siblings and fellow citizens, not because we have Jesus as Lord, as he previously stated, but now because Jesus has life and death power over all, and because He is our Creator. That means the members of the entire—human—race are siblings and should consider each other fellow citizens of Christ's kingdom. But as we pointed out, he already said:

> But we are brothers and sisters of all Christians around the world who proclaim Jesus as the Christ. We haven't been given the authority to delegitimize the sonship, daughtership, or siblingship of Christ-followers who differ from us in belief and behavior.[27]

Here he is using a different paradigm—those who have accepted Christ—but he also says we are all brothers and sisters because Jesus created us all and has power over life and death. Which one and which way does he believe? Dr. Bryan seems confused in what he himself believes.

Consider the following statement from the Spirit of Prophecy:

> When our ministers seek to present something that is new and strange to the common people, they are not following the custom of Christ. Sometimes the things they endeavor to present they do not themselves understand, and they lead minds away from the path of truth and righteousness. Self, self! When will self die! And when shall we learn what it means to follow in the footsteps of Jesus! (*Australian Union Conference Record*, January 6, 1908)

Dr. Bryan has made all the following claims on pages 34 and 35 of *The Green Cord Dream*:

- Every human being is a "fellow citizen and subject of the kingdom" because Jesus has life and death control over every human being.
- Every human being is a "fellow citizen and subject of the kingdom" because Jesus created every human being.
- All human beings are "siblings," meaning we are all brothers and sisters because Jesus created every human being.
- We have no right to judge who is and who isn't a brother, sister, or sibling because we have all been created by the same God.

27 Ibid., 35.

- We have no right to judge who is and who isn't a brother, sister, or sibling among those who have claimed that "Jesus is their Lord," even if their beliefs and behavior differ from ours.
- Although we can't judge, we need to hope that those who don't know God will come to know Him, and in the meantime, we must consider them all siblings and citizens of the kingdom.

There is more confusion, but I don't want to further complicate things. According to these expressions, the only logical conclusion that can be drawn is that every human being is a brother, sister, sibling, fellow citizen, and heir of the kingdom because Jesus made us all and has life and death power over us all. See below:

> Recognizing that He has jurisdiction and life-or-death power over every human being, then we should see one another as *fellow citizens, subjects of the same kingdom.* (Switching metaphors): If all of us are children of God because *He created all of us, then we are … siblings*! [28]

Along with this claim, comes the next contradicting statement:

> But we are brothers and sisters of all Christians around the world who proclaim Jesus as the Christ. We haven't been given the authority to delegitimize the son-ship, daughter-ship, or sibling-ship of Christ's followers who differ from us in belief or behavior. [29]

After telling us to call every human being a brother and sister in the Lord because Jesus created us all and has power over life and death, he switches his reasoning over to whether they are brother, sister, or sibling due to the fact that they have called Jesus their Lord, as we do, and says we should treat them:

> "As beloved siblings whom we hope will come to know God." [30]

---

28 Bryan, *The Green Cord Dream,* 34, emphasis added.

29 Ibid., 35, emphasis added.

30 Ibid.

This has been presented in a most confusing manner. These are the same people Dr. Bryan said we are to treat as brothers and sisters because they are Christians, but here he claims that they don't know God! HELP!

So, in all this we have covered the entire human population and are counseled to consider them all brothers and sisters in the Lord. This theology leaves the Seventh-day Adventist Church without a mission; without any reason for the first, second, or third angels' messages. Why? Because according to Dr. Bryan, everyone in the entire world is already brothers, sisters, fellow citizens, and members of the kingdom of God, for all are "one,"—just as the theologians who developed the emerging theology would have it, and dare I say, just as Satan himself would have it, for it brings a halt to the sounding of the loud cry, and a people prepared for Jesus' return, that which Dr. Bryan claimed earlier was "darkness."

The very thing that Jesus was trying to do during the Great Disappointment—have people check their heart for readiness for a soon second coming, as was just stated: "I saw the wisdom of God in proving His people and giving them a searching test. (*Early Writings*, 236)

Let's search Inspiration and discover real theological truth instead of reading human theories learned in the schools of Egypt. Inspiration tells us that Jesus does not reign in the hearts of sinners, those who do not strive to live righteously, according to God's law. Once again, the author's confusion results from not reading the inspired counsel we have in the Spirit of Prophecy; counsel that plainly supports the truth that only those who follow after righteousness have Jesus living in their hearts, and it is Satan who dwells in the hearts of all others.

> In *Living Temple* the assertion is made that God is in the flower, in the leaf, in the sinner. But God does not live in the sinner. The Word declares that He abides only in the hearts of those who love Him and do righteousness. God does not abide in the heart of the sinner; it is the enemy who abides there. (*Sermons and Talks*, vol. 1, 343)

Also:

> Whatever may be the ecstasies of religious feeling, Jesus cannot abide in the heart that disregards the divine law. God will honor those only who honor Him. (*The Sanctified Life*, 92)

Righteousness is defined in Scripture as "all thy commandments" in Psalm 119:172: "My tongue shall speak of thy word: for all thy commandments are righteousness."

It is those who do righteousness, or who are following the light Jesus has shined on them, who have Jesus living in their hearts, while those who do not do righteousness have Satan living in their hearts. It is, of course, impossible for us to judge individuals and see into their hearts, but it is without doubt an error and a kind of pantheism to instruct us that we should relate to every member of Protestant churches who proclaim Jesus as Lord, and every other human being on earth as fellow citizens, Christian brothers and sisters, and members of the kingdom of God.

> Not everyone that saith unto me, Lord, Lord, shall enter into the kingdom of heaven; but he that doeth the will of my Father which is in heaven,"—the will made known in the Ten Commandments, given in Eden when the morning stars sang together, and all the sons of God shouted for joy, and spoken with an audible voice from Sinai. "Many will say to me in that day, Lord, Lord, have we not prophesied in thy name? and in thy name have cast out devils? and in thy name done many wonderful works? And then will I profess unto them, I never knew you: depart from me, ye that work iniquity." Many mighty works are done under the inspiration of Satan, and these works will be more and more apparent in the last days. (*The Review and Herald*, May 7, 1901)

These are churches that we know from Inspiration have Satan as their leader, and are churches filled mostly with those who are rebelling against righteousness, and have openly rejected God's law, warring against it. This means that they are warring against righteousness, for Scripture teaches that "all thy commandments are righteousness" (Psalm 119:172). The spiritual teaching and outlook reveal a dangerous lack of discernment, a danger that sweeps the rug out from under the foundational teachings of the Seventh-day Adventist Church—the three angels' messages. Once again, this error in thinking could have been avoided if counsel was from the Bible and the Spirit of Prophecy instead of seeking the instruction from the schools of Babylon.

Allow me to stress once again for the sake of not wanting to be misunderstood that there are true, Spirit-led Christians spread among the various churches in the world today who have a saving relationship with

God, are members of His church, and are truly our brothers and sisters. These people, including any others who respond to the call to proclaim the three angels' messages, are the primary purpose of our outreach and, for that matter, our lives. But if one fast forwards to the very end of time, the Spirit of Prophecy teaching that the denominated Protestant churches are under the influence of satanic power and falsely believe that God is working for them when He is not; that the vast majority of these people are agents of Satan and are at war against God's law fits with the scriptural model. There is a group who, in the end, choose to slay God's true people in the final crisis. Theologically, are these who we are to join with and consider brothers and sisters in the Lord? Or are they those who we are to give our lives to, bringing to them an understanding of Jesus according to Scripture and the Spirit of Prophecy?

> I saw that God has honest children among the nominal Adventists and the fallen churches, and before the plagues shall be poured out, ministers and people will be called out from these churches and will gladly receive the truth. Satan knows this; and before the loud cry of the third angel is given, he raises an excitement in these religious bodies, that those who have rejected the truth may think that God is with them. He hopes to deceive the honest and lead them to think that God is still working for the churches. But the light will shine, and all who are honest will leave the fallen churches, and take their stand with the remnant. (*Early Writings*, 261)

Notice that Satan will raise excitement among these churches so that they believe God is working with them, when He is not. A right relationship with the inspired writings God has given to us to avoid these pitfalls is key.

In this statement, Ellen White is saying that the fallen churches will be deceived right up until the time of the loud cry, and that this deception will only become worse as Satan ushers in a false revival just prior to that event. True believers will be called out before the plagues are poured out. Again, this demonstrates that there is never a time when the Protestant churches come back into favor with God. They are deceived and under satanic influence now, the daughters of Babylon, and will be deceived until the close of probation. This point must be understood and accepted to be able to discern the truth concerning the author's counsel to treat those in these churches as fellow Christians because they claim Jesus as Lord. We read:

> I saw that as the Jews crucified Jesus, so the nominal churches had crucified these messages, and therefore they have no knowledge of the way into the most holy, and they cannot be benefited by the intercession of Jesus there … they offer up their useless prayers to the apartment which Jesus has left; and Satan, pleased with the deception, assumes a religious character, and leads the minds of these professed Christians to himself, working with his power, his signs and lying wonders, to fasten them in his snare. … Satan deceives some with Spiritualism. He also comes as an angel of light and spreads his influence over the land by means of false reformations. The churches are elated, and consider that God is working marvelously for them, when it is the work of another spirit. The excitement will die away and leave the world and the church in a worse condition than before. (*Early Writings*, 261)

Notice that Ellen White calls the members of these churches, in general, "professed Christians." There are disparities with true brothers and sisters and professed Christians. Do you see the problem?

The "nominal Adventists" were those in the Advent/Millerite movement who never accepted the Sabbath truth and the Spirit of Prophecy following the Great Disappointment. They formed their own Sunday-keeping churches. All other Protestant denominations would be those described above as the "fallen" churches. Every one of them had the opportunity to receive the message of truth that was presented to them, but they rejected those messages.

The theology expressed is reminiscent of Roman Catholic theology, and contradicts our belief that we are the remnant with Christ as our leader, while the other Protestant churches are the fallen daughters of Babylon, deceived, having Satan as their leader. We love them, but they are not Christian siblings under the Lord's leadership; neither are they sons and daughters of God at this time. They are deceived and fallen because their denominational Protestant churches rejected the first and second angels' messages, and they have chosen to remain fastened in that deception. According to the Spirit of Prophecy, this is the reason Satan rules over these denominations, and why Ellen White refers to them as professed Christians. These professed Christians will one day either accept the truth, put away sin and be persecuted by Satan, or they will be taken in by Satan's snares.

> Through deceptive means and unseen channels, Satan is working to strengthen his authority and to place obstacles in the way of God's people, that souls may not be freed from his power and gathered under the banner of Christ. By his deceptions he is seeking to allure souls from Christ, and those who are not established upon the truth will surely be taken in his snare. And those whom he cannot lead into sin he will persecute, as the Jews did Christ. (*Testimonies for the Church,* vol. 5, 295)

The Lord allowed Satan to take control of the Protestant churches when they rejected the Adventist's proclamation of the second angel's message during the summer of 1844. They have remained there ever since, and will remain under Satan's control until probation closes. Today, most members of these churches remain deceived, and although claiming to be Christians, lead lives consistent with those who have rejected the law of God—our only measure of righteousness. They are members of the churches we believe are the daughters of Babylon. How else can we judge the Protestant churches other than by Scripture?

> To the law and to the testimony: if they speak not according to this word, it is because there is no light in them. (Isaiah 8:20)

The control of the Protestant churches has been Satan's objective for a long time, and he does not deviate from this objective:

> History repeats itself. The same masterful mind that plotted against the faithful in ages past is now at work to gain control of the Protestant churches, that through them he may condemn and put to death all who will not worship the idol sabbath. We have not to battle with man, as it may appear. We wrestle not against flesh and blood, but against principalities, against powers, against the rulers of the darkness of this world, against spiritual wickedness in high places. But if the people of God will put their trust in Him, and by faith rely upon His power, the devices of Satan will be defeated in our time as signally as in the days of Mordecai. (*The Signs of the Times,* November 8, 1899)

These are the churches we are to call God's people out of, and they are the objects of our mission, but they are not churches filled with people we should call brothers and sisters in Jesus. To do so leavens the message of the three angels of Revelation 14 and is the reason the teaching in the book *The Green Cord Dream* is so dangerous. If this were the case, if they were truly sons and daughters of God, siblings, as the author suggests, why would they need to be called out of, or separate from, anything? If his beliefs were correct, there is no Babylon for anyone to be called out of, for they are already true Christians, citizens of the kingdom. There would be no need for the three angels' messages—there would be no need for the Seventh-day Adventist Church.

There is danger in this theology. It can eventually render the three angels' messages worthless, useless, while in reality it is the very heart of our movement and the very message the Lord gave the Seventh-day Adventist Church to proclaim to the world.

Chapter Eight:

Emergent Plans

We need to look more thoroughly at the article written by the author that we briefly examined in Chapter 6, The One Project. The following is an excerpt from that article in *Adventist Today*, Winter 2009, page 10. This was written while the author was the pastor for mission and ministry at the Collegedale Church of Seventh-day Adventists in Collegedale, Tennessee. It should be noted that publication called *Adventist Today* is a liberal SDA publication.

> I've talked with enough children of missionaries and students who themselves were missionaries to know that exposure to the thrills and trials of hands-on ministry is powerful. *Encapsulation* is the word theologian Scot McKnight gives it. You are removed from the protected, pampered life and thrown into it.
>
> Why can't we, the Great Advent Movement, do whatever is financially necessary to make this happen? Or are we simply going to continue to instruct students in desk-and-chalkboard or pulpit-and-pew environments about the "28" and Adventist Heritage? While head knowledge about fundamental beliefs and denominational history is important, what are these without the spiritual cardio of missional exercise? I believe a major paradigm jolt is in order for a church that is scrambling to find safety as the tectonic plates of culture quake beneath us. We spend some 40 percent of our tithe dollars on Christian education in North America, and we've got a 15-year age gap between Average American and Average Adventist! Something's got to change.
>
> The impact of teenage service is not simply so that 25 years later the initial investment finds dividends. We need 18- to 22-year-olds trained so that *23- to 35-year-olds* can start *leading* the church.

Right away. Then. Now. We need pastorates, pulpits, committees, boards, and initiatives *filled* with *very young* adults. Not tokens. Not the one 27-year-old who is really a 77-year-old in a 20-something body. We need holy and hungry, spiritual and sassy, Christ-centered and creative young people. We need the kind who know a lot about the Bible *and* the culture. We need those who are friends of Jesus and who can easily make friends with those *outside* the church. A "piece of the pie" was okay in 1990. But times have changed, for the worse. Now we must give them the *keys to the bakery* before we have to put a going-out-of business sign on the window.

Faith, Hope, and Love: These three I keep in my heart, mind, and soul.

I have faith that God has important work he still wants to do through the Adventist Church.

I have hope that church leaders will recognize the power of healing change over catastrophic calcification.

I have love for this spiritual family—the Seventh-day Adventist Church—around the world, but especially in America, where the Spirit conceived a community of high scriptural regard, cross bearing discipleship, Sabbatical celebration, and, yes, blessed hope. Can God use anyone to do the work of these important times? Sure. I say: why not us?

Alex Bryan is the pastor for mission and ministry at the Collegedale Church of Seventh-day Adventists in Collegedale, Tennessee. [31]

Notes and bibliography for above article:

[1] Tom Sine, *The New Conspirators: Creating the Future One Mustard Seed at a Time* (Downers Grove, Ill.: Intervarsity Press: 2008), p. 205.

[2] Leonard Sweet, *The Church of the Perfect Storm* (Nashville: Abingdon Press, 2008), p. 14.

[3] Methodism, a parent of the Adventist Church, is on course to shut down its last congregation in the year 2090—just 82 years from now.

31 Bryan, "The End of American Adventism?", *10.*

Accessed at http://umportal.org/print_article.asp?id+4270 in an article by Donald W. Haynes, retired clergy member of the Western North Carolina Conference.

[4] *Christianity Today*, August 2008.

[5] Alex Bryan, *The Local Church Is The Church. Period. Adventist Review*, March 19, 1998, pp. 8–13 (can be accessed through the *Adventist Review* online archival system).

[6] Malcolm Bull and Keith Lockhart, *Seeking a Sanctuary: Seventh-day Adventism and the American Dream* (Bloomington, Ind.: Indiana University Press, 1989), pp. 290–301.

[7] I recently saw an interview with founder and CEO Wendy Kopp. The lifelong impact on those who serve in the program is enormous. See www.teachforamerica.org for more information.

[8] Scot McKnight, *Turning to Jesus: The Sociology of Conversion in the Gospels* (Louisville, Ky.: Westminster John Knox Press, 2002), pp. 92–98.

We will limit our concerns to three areas. Let us begin with the offensive and distasteful use of "the 28," in reference to our fundamental beliefs.

> "Or are we simply going to continue to instruct students in desk-and-chalkboard or pulpit-and-pew environments about 'the 28' and Adventist Heritage?"[32]

Those who stayed together after the Great Disappointment wrestled with Scripture through sleepless nights, praying and pleading with God for light concerning their past experience. In this process, studying God's Word and searching with all their hearts for the precious shining light in the pillars of our faith, which the author refers to as those "28," Ellen White could not participate and called the experience one of the saddest of her life.

The Lord prevented His messenger from being able to join with her Christian family and share the joy in discovering new light, and partake of the excitement of her friends. They were discovering the truths which corrected the errors in the existing Protestant teachings and more. God was opening their minds to new lines of truth, lines which connected

32 Ibid.

Scripture's message together in ways it had never been connected before, including the explanation and reasons for the Great Disappointment. The Lord verified their searching through Inspiration, but never wanted it to be claimed that Ellen White was the originator of any of the new truths discovered. For this reason, Ellen White's mind was closed to these new discoveries until the truth was discovered by those doing the searching. Ellen White then had revelations to verify the truths discovered.

Those "28," as the author refers to them, are the result of the Lord calling His final remnant church out of Babylon. For their effort and for these new discoveries to be belittled is very offensive to those of us who understand just how important they are. They are Christ, for He is discovered, and known, through His teachings.

By ridicule and sarcasm the author reveals his own lack of understanding of what he refers to as "the 28." Instead of being so cocky and self-assured, he should be humbled and consider that he is presenting a theology that is destructive and false. For example:

> Or are we simply going to continue to instruct students in desk-and-chalkboard or pulpit-and-pew environments about the "28" and *Adventist Heritage*?... I believe a major paradigm jolt is in order for a church that is scrambling to find safety as the tectonic plates of culture quake beneath us.[33]

Perhaps we should remember that just prior to Dr. Bryan's writing this article in *Adventist Today*, he resigned his employment with God's church, totally separating himself by his decision to pastor a new congregation in a Sunday-keeping church. His new church was an Independent Evangelical Church. After he returned and claimed to have "learned lessons," one might have expected to see more of a humble, repentant attitude and perhaps an attempt to reclaim those who were lost by his temporary wayward ministry but this was not the case.

He is a talented writer, attractive to the young people who are in the bull's eye of the targeted audience, but in the above reference he refers to God's church, the Seventh-day Adventist Church, as "a church." This may be his estimation of the Seventh-day Adventist Church. It's just another church; a church that might make it if it adopts the radical reforms he suggests. This writing appears to contain resentment toward the church of

33 Ibid.

God, and against those young people (GYC) who are meeting every year by the thousands, striving for revival by returning to those "28." They also sound proud and self-assured, not as though they come from one who has truly learned lessons from having temporarily left God's church.

1. Eleven times he uses the terms *I, I believe, we, we need, I say, I have, I keep, I've talked, my heart*. You get the point, I'm sure.
2. You will notice the concepts are regarded as "revolutionary," calling for a change in the entire church. A quick look at the bibliography and references in *The Green Cord Dream*, as well as in many books claimed to be life changing and often commended at The One Project meetings, will reveal that the philosophy is absolutely dependent on non-Adventist, emergent church authors. This is an expected outcome, as Dr. Bryan received his doctor of ministry in leadership and emerging culture from George Fox University under the tutelage of Dr. Leonard Sweet and other emergent church leaders.
3. Most troubling are these two comments, written while he was being mentored by Leonard Sweet:
   - A. "Now we must give them the *keys to the bakery* before we have to put a going-out-of business sign on the window."
   - B. "I have faith that God has important work he still wants to do through the Adventist Church."[34]

The thoughts expressed in these two sentences once again reveal a lack of understanding of the mission and purpose of the Seventh-day Adventist Church. Apparently, the author is not aware of, or does not believe that we are never "going out of business." He would know this, and would never have said the things he said, if he understood and believed in the Spirit of Prophecy. Instead, he uses it when it fits into his agenda, and it appears he believes and relies upon it, but if he truly did rely on it for his understanding of our mission, he would not write or think the way he does.

For example: When he says that he has "faith that God has important work he still wants to do through the Adventist Church," he reveals that he does not understand our identity or mission. He has not grasped the truth that there will be no others in this world who will give the three

34 Ibid.

angels' messages and who will prepare a people to be translated when Jesus returns. Our church—God's remnant Seventh-day Adventist Church, may appear as if it is about to fall, "but it does not fall." We go on to give the loud cry found in Revelation 18:1–6, and "This is the message given by God to be sounded forth in the loud cry of the third angel" (*Testimonies for the Church*, vol. 8, 118).

It results in exposing the sins of Babylon and her daughters, the daughters with whom all erroneous movements are infatuated. These are the daughters of the papacy who lost their status as God's people back in the mid-1800s, when they rejected the first and second angels' messages. This is what Inspiration teaches us, and we need to make a choice either to accept this truth as expressed in the Spirit of Prophecy, or to reject it as a fable. It appears that those whose beliefs we are studying do not believe this truth, for they chose to attend these schools and bring their false teachings back to our churches and schools.

The author's problem, like most others who share their opinions and write for *Adventist Today*, is that they have not gained their understanding, or made plans for their future, by relying upon the special Inspiration the Lord gave the Seventh-day Adventist Church through the ministry of Ellen White, but have depended on the emergent teachers and prophets of Egypt (Babylon). Like those who rebelled in Israel of old, recorded in Isaiah chapter 30, their church—Israel (the Seventh-day Adventist Church of today) did not profit them (Isaiah 30:5). These people follow after the teachings of Egypt:

> Woe to the rebellious children, saith the Lord, that take counsel, but not of me; and that cover with a covering, but not of my spirit, that they may add sin to sin:
>
> That walk to go down into Egypt, and have not asked at my mouth; to strengthen themselves in the strength of Pharaoh, and to trust in the shadow of Egypt!
>
> Therefore shall the strength of Pharaoh be your shame, and the trust in the shadow of Egypt your confusion.
>
> For his princes were at Zoan, and his ambassadors came to Hanes.

> They were all ashamed of a people that could not profit them, nor be an help nor profit, but a shame, and also a reproach. (Isaiah 30:1–5)

Shame may be the motivation for going outside of their own church to learn new methods and practices, emphasizing emerging church teachings. As the Spirit of Prophecy says, "So long as they refuse to heed the warnings given them, the spell that is upon them cannot be broken" (*Spaulding and Magan Collection*, 465).

What is the importance placed on "other teachings" by the author and many of his colleagues who attended George Fox University, teachings they could not find in their own church? So, they went elsewhere, and have learned the Roman Catholic teaching of the emerging church, choosing to depend on non-Adventist mystics to develop their theology—the mysticism of papal Rome.

We must all understand and value the matter of the shaking in Adventism, a reality that prepares the church to allow the Lord to do His miraculous work through them for Jesus' return. Having already begun, when it takes place in earnest, it is brought about by the very false teachings this movement often supports.

How sad that those who are spreading this false theology have not grasped the historical fact that the Lord was in control of the events of those times, and that they have incorrectly attributed the misunderstanding of Scripture of those in the movement to some other evil influence upon them, as they refer to the movement as "failure," "darkness," and "error." Those who participated in the movement who were truly following the Lord's lead claimed that it was the most exciting and wonderful time of their lives; a time of constant victory and the attending presence of the Spirit of God, not one of failure and darkness.

My dear Adventist family, although I admit to a degree of righteous indignation because of the potential for innocent people to follow these false teachings, my heart still goes out to those who are spreading this deception throughout the church. They are part of our family also, and I do constantly lift them before the Lord, pleading for their deliverance from the power that holds them in this deception, and do ask you to join with me in this endeavor.

Satan has a way of dragging those whom he can beyond the point of no return, while at the same time convincing them that they have not gone too far. It is one of his age-old and greatest deceptions. We must pray for one another without ceasing, that the limits are not pushed in any of our misunderstandings and erroneous decisions. And as for this confused theology, prayer for and by those involved, that the pure application of Scripture and the Spirit of Prophecy will replace the guidance of mystic advisors, is vital. Pleading for light and truth, employing the Inspiration God has given His remnant church, rather than the darkness of fallen Babylon's mystics and spiritualists, will impart life itself.

It is time now, as we have presented most of the facts, to see how Inspiration describes the beginning of our movement. This next section contains selected quotes from Inspiration that will help us to truly understand our beginnings, for it is an inspired account of what took place. It is recorded in *Life Sketches*, 59–68. You will see from Inspiration that there is no record of failure, darkness, and error, as in the record of *The Green Cord Dream*. The compilation begins after the Lord did not return in 1843, the first date they set for His return.

Hope Renewed

> Our hopes now centered on the coming of the Lord in 1844. This was also the time for the message of the second angel, who, flying through the midst of heaven, cried, "Babylon is fallen, is fallen, that great city" Revelation 14:8. That message was first proclaimed by the servants of God in the summer of 1844. As a result, many left the fallen churches. In connection with this message the "midnight cry" [See Matthew 25:1–13.] was given: "Behold, the Bridegroom cometh; go ye out to meet Him." In every part of the land light was given concerning this message, and the cry aroused thousands. It went from city to city, from village to village, and into the remote country regions. It reached the learned and talented, as well as the obscure and humble.
>
> This was the happiest year of my life. My heart was full of glad expectation; but I felt great pity and anxiety for those who were in discouragement and had no hope in Jesus. We united, as a people, in earnest prayer for a true experience and the unmistakable evidence of our acceptance with God.

A Trial of Faith

We needed great patience, for the scoffers were many. We were frequently greeted by scornful references to our former disappointment. The orthodox churches used every means to prevent the belief in Christ's soon coming from spreading. No liberty was granted in their meetings to those who dared mention a hope of the soon coming of Christ. Professed lovers of Jesus scornfully rejected the tidings that He whom they claimed as their best Friend was soon to visit them. They were excited and angered against those who proclaimed the news of His coming, and who rejoiced that they should speedily behold Him in His glory.

A Period of Preparation

Every moment seemed to me of the utmost importance. I felt that we were doing work for eternity, and that the careless and uninterested were in the greatest peril. My faith was unclouded, and I appropriated to myself the precious promises of Jesus. He had said to His disciples, "Ask, and ye shall receive." I firmly believed that whatever I asked in accordance with the will of God, would certainly be granted to me. I sank in humility at the feet of Jesus, with my heart in harmony with His will.

I often visited families, and engaged in earnest prayer with those who were oppressed by fears and despondency. My faith was so strong that I never doubted for a moment that God would answer my prayers. Without a single exception, the blessing and peace of Jesus rested upon us in answer to our humble petitions, and the hearts of the despairing ones were made joyful by light and hope.
With diligent searching of heart and humble confessions, we came prayerfully up to the time of expectation. Every morning we felt that it was our first work to secure the evidence that our lives were right before God. We realized that if we were not advancing in holiness, we were sure to retrograde. Our interest for one another increased; we prayed much with and for one another. We assembled in the orchards and groves to commune with God and to offer up our petitions to Him, feeling more fully in His presence when surrounded by His natural works. The joys of salvation were more

necessary to us than our food and drink. If clouds obscured our minds, we dared not rest or sleep till they were swept away by the consciousness of our acceptance with the Lord.

The Passing of the Time

The waiting people of God approached the hour when they fondly hoped their joys would be complete in the coming of the Savior. But the time again passed unmarked by the advent of Jesus. It was a bitter disappointment that fell upon the little flock whose faith had been so strong and whose hope had been so high. But we were surprised that we felt so free in the Lord, and were so strongly sustained by His strength and grace.

The experience of the former year was, however, repeated to a greater extent. A large class renounced their faith. Some who had been very confident were so deeply wounded in their pride that they felt like fleeing from the world. Like Jonah, they complained of God, and chose death rather than life. Those who had built their faith upon the evidence of others, and not upon the word of God, were now as ready to again change their views. This second great test revealed a mass of worthless drift that had been drawn into the strong current of the advent faith, and been borne along for a time with the true believers and earnest workers.

We were disappointed, but not disheartened. We resolved to refrain from murmuring at the trying ordeal by which the Lord was purging us from the dross and refining us like gold in the furnace; to submit patiently to the process of purifying that God deemed needful for us; and to wait with patient hope for the Saviour to redeem His tried and faithful ones.

We were firm in the belief that the preaching of definite time was of God. It was this that led men to search the Bible diligently, discovering truths they had not before perceived. Jonah was sent of God to proclaim in the streets of Nineveh that within forty days the city would be overthrown; but God accepted the humiliation of the Ninevites, and extended their period of probation. Yet the message that Jonah brought was sent of God, and Nineveh was tested according to His will. The world looked upon our hope as a delusion, and our disappointment as its consequent failure; but though we were mistaken in the event that was to occur at that period, there was no failure in reality of the vision that seemed to tarry.

Those who had looked for the coming of the Lord were not without comfort. They had obtained valuable knowledge in the searching of the Word. The plan of salvation was plainer to their understanding. Every day they discovered new beauties in the sacred pages, and a wonderful harmony running through all, one scripture explaining another, and no word used in vain.

Our disappointment was not as great as that of the disciples. When the Son of man rode triumphantly into Jerusalem, they expected Him to be crowned king. The people flocked from all the region about, and cried, "Hosanna to the Son of David." Matthew 21:9. And when the priests and elders besought Jesus to still the multitude, He declared that if they should hold their peace, even the stones would cry out, for prophecy must be fulfilled. Yet in a few days these very disciples saw their beloved Master, whom they believed would reign on David's throne, stretched upon the cruel cross above the mocking, taunting Pharisees. Their high hopes were disappointed, and the darkness of death closed about them. Yet Christ was true to His promises. Sweet was the consolation He gave His people, rich the reward of the true and faithful.

Mr. Miller and those who were in union with him supposed that the cleansing of the sanctuary spoken of in Daniel 8:14 meant the purifying of the earth by fire prior to its becoming the abode of the saints. This was to take place at the second advent of Christ; therefore we looked for that event at the end of the 2300 days, or years. But after our disappointment the Scriptures were carefully searched, with prayer and earnest thought; and after a period of suspense, light poured in upon our darkness; doubt and uncertainty were swept away.

Instead of the prophecy of Daniel 8:14 referring to the purifying of the earth, it was now plain that it pointed to the closing work of our High Priest in heaven, the finishing of the atonement, and the preparing of the people to abide the day of His coming

Chap. VII—My First Vision

It was not long after the passing of the time in 1844, that my first vision was given me. I was visiting Mrs. Haines at Portland, a dear sister in Christ, whose heart was knit with mine; five of us, all women, were kneeling quietly at the family altar. While we were praying, the power of God came upon me as I had never felt it before.

I seemed to be surrounded with light, and to be rising higher and higher from the earth. I turned to look for the advent people in the world, but could not find them, when a voice said to me, "Look again, and look a little higher." At this I raised my eyes, and saw a straight and narrow path, cast up high above the world. On this path the advent people were traveling to the city which was at the farther end of the path. (*Life Sketches*, 59–64)

The midnight cry (The supposed failure and darkness was the light of the midnight cry, which illuminated their future path; see the midnight cry above.), given during the summer of 1844, resulted in the happiest year of Ellen White's life, and is the supposed failure and darkness referred to in *The Green Cord Dream*.

They had a bright light set up behind them at the beginning of the path, which an angel told me was the "midnight cry." This light shone all along the path, and gave light for their feet, so that they might not stumble.

If they kept their eyes fixed on Jesus, who was just before them, leading them to the city, they were safe. But soon some grew weary, and said the city was a great way off, and they expected to have entered it before. Then Jesus would encourage them by raising His glorious right arm, and from His arm came a light which waved over the advent band, and they shouted "Alleluia!" (Ibid., 64)

This vision is extremely important. There were those who denied that they were being led by God in giving the message leading up to October 22, 1844. In Ellen White's vision, the light illuminating the future was the light of the midnight cry, the message given during the summer of 1844, yet reaching all the way to the second coming of Jesus. Ellen White was given this vision after October 22, 1844, to encourage the disappointed Adventists and to show them the way into the city of God. They saw the hand of God in the mistakes they had made and God did not leave them distraught, with the feelings of "failure," "error," "sadness," and "darkness." This was not the experience the Adventists had. God loved and cared for them as He tested them. In their disappointment, He encouraged them through the gift of prophecy.

Today, unbelief is being expressed when calling that same midnight cry "failure" and "darkness."

> Others rashly denied the light behind them, and said that it was not God that had led them out so far. The light behind them went out, leaving their feet in perfect darkness, and they stumbled and lost sight of the mark and of Jesus, and fell off the path down into the dark and wicked world below.
>
> Soon we heard the voice of God like many waters, which gave us the day and hour of Jesus' coming. The living saints, 144,000 in number, knew and understood the voice, while the wicked thought it was thunder and an earthquake. When God spoke the time, He poured upon us the Holy Ghost, and our faces began to light up and shine with the glory of God, as Moses' did when he came down from Mount Sinai.
>
> The 144,000 were all sealed and perfectly united. On their foreheads was written, "God, New Jerusalem," and a glorious star containing Jesus' new name. At our happy, holy state the wicked were enraged, and would rush violently up to lay hands on us to thrust us into prison, when we would stretch forth the hand in the name of the Lord, and they would fall helpless to the ground. Then it was that the synagogue of Satan knew that God had loved us who could wash one another's feet, and salute the brethren with a holy kiss, and they worshiped at our feet.

Soon our eyes were drawn to the east, for a small black cloud had appeared, about half as large as a man's hand, which we all knew was the sign of the Son of man. We all in solemn silence gazed on the cloud as it drew nearer, and became lighter, glorious, and still more glorious, till it was a great white cloud. The bottom appeared like fire; a rainbow was over the cloud, while around it were ten thousand angels, singing a most lovely song; and upon it sat the Son of man. His hair was white and curly, and lay on His shoulders; and upon His head were many crowns. His feet had the appearance of fire; in His right hand was a sharp sickle; in His left, a silver trumpet. His eyes were as a flame of fire, which searched His children through and through. Then all faces gathered paleness, and those that God had rejected gathered blackness. Then we all cried out: "Who shall be able to stand? Is my robe spotless?" Then the angels ceased to sing, and there was some time of awful silence, when Jesus spoke: "Those who have clean hands and pure hearts shall be able to stand; My grace is sufficient for you." At this our faces lighted up, and joy filled every heart. And the angels struck a note higher and sang again, while the cloud drew still nearer the earth.

Then Jesus' silver trumpet sounded, as He descended on the cloud, wrapped in flames of fire. He gazed on the graves of the sleeping saints, then raised His eyes and hands to heaven, and cried, "Awake! awake! awake! ye that sleep in the dust, and arise." Then there was a mighty earthquake. The graves opened, and the dead came up clothed with immortality. The 144,000 shouted "Alleluia!" as they recognized their friends who had been torn from them by death, and in the same moment we were changed and caught up together with them to meet the Lord in the air.

We all entered the cloud together, and were seven days ascending to the sea of glass, when Jesus brought the crowns, and with His own right hand placed them on our heads. He gave us harps of gold and palms of victory. Here on the sea of glass the 144,000 stood in a perfect square. Some of them had very bright crowns, others not so bright. Some crowns appeared heavy with stars, while others had but few. All were perfectly satisfied with their crowns. And they were all clothed with a glorious white mantle from their shoulders to their feet. Angels were all about us as we marched over the sea of glass to the gate of the city. Jesus raised His mighty, glorious arm, laid hold of the pearly gate, swung it back on its glittering hinges, and said to us, "You have washed your robes in My blood, stood stiffly for My truth, enter in." We all marched in and felt that we had a perfect right in the city.

Here we saw the tree of life and the throne of God. Out of the throne came a pure river of water, and on either side of the river was the tree of life. On one side of the river was a trunk of a tree, and a trunk on the other side of the river, both of pure, transparent gold. At first I thought I saw two trees. I looked again, and saw that they were united at the top in one tree. So it was the tree of life on either side of the river of life. Its branches bowed to the place where we stood, and the fruit was glorious; it looked like gold mixed with silver.

We all went under the tree, and sat down to look at the glory of the place, when Brethren Fitch and Stockman, who had preached the gospel of the kingdom, and whom God had laid in the grave to save them, came up to us and asked us what we had passed through while they were sleeping. We tried to call up our greatest trials, but they looked so small compared with the far more exceeding and eternal weight of glory that surrounded us, that we could not speak them out, and we all cried out, "Alleluia! heaven is cheap enough!" and we touched our glorious harps and made heaven's arches ring.

After I came out of vision, everything seemed changed; a gloom was spread over all that I beheld. Oh, how dark this world looked to me! I wept when I found myself here, and felt homesick. I had seen a better world, and it had spoiled this for me.

I related this vision to the believers in Portland, who had full confidence that it was from God. They all believed that God had chosen this way, after the Great Disappointment in October, to comfort and strengthen His people. The Spirit of the Lord attended the testimony, and the solemnity of eternity rested upon us. An unspeakable awe filled me, that I, so young and feeble, should be chosen as the instrument by which God would give light to His people.

While under the power of the Lord, I was filled with joy, seeming to be surrounded by holy angels in the glorious courts of heaven, where all is peace and gladness; and it was a sad and bitter change to wake up to the realities of mortal life" (Ibid., 64–67).

How God Works in History

We have shown in this chapter how our movement was in the order of God, a movement that He was constantly guiding, including the mistakes that were a part of His plan, and how He withheld the light that led to the wrong interpretation of Scripture. Since sin began, this is how God has always worked with His people.

As we already examined in Chapter 7, God has always allowed truth to unfold, which inherently allows for mistakes to be made when we attempt to understand truths that God does not yet desire us to understand. This is not "failure" or "darkness," but is the natural result of how God works with His church. It is His will and is in accordance with how He has always led His people. Often, even when His people interpret things incorrectly, God is guiding them through their misunderstanding, fulfilling His will as revealed in the prediction of the Triumphal Entry in Zechariah 9:9. His thoughts and ways are far above ours, and we need to be extremely careful not to try to make God be the way we want Him to be, instead of the way He really is.

This was Ignatius Loyola's error. He would not accept Inspiration's revelation of the character and attributes of God, as seems to be the resistance of many, including a number of leaders in this current movement. While Luther sought inspiration, discovering salvation by grace through faith, Loyola returned to Babylon and found the God he wanted—the one he insisted on having, instead of the God of heaven. This deception, created by Ignatius Loyola, permeates any teaching that seeks truth by returning to Babylon in whatever form instead of that which was provided by God Himself, His inspired sources. It pushes forward the malignant notion that God's attributes are the ones desired, true or not.

Now we will examine one last topic. Dr. Bryan calls for "revolution" (*Revolution: Finding Vibrant Faith Beyond the Walls of the Church*, by David Kinnamen, recommended in *The Green Cord Dream*) in a failing church. He believes it to be a church that has lost its way, just one of many churches that God has in the world (which he illustrates by showing many puzzle pieces in a glass), and one that he worries will not make it if it doesn't accept his suggestions for change for "revolution." He claims over and over that the young people in our church need to take over by getting themselves placed on all the important church boards so they can be the decision makers of the future.

The title of his book, *The Green Cord Dream*, suggests trust and reliance upon the Spirit of Prophecy, but it paints the erroneous picture of a church that began in failure and darkness, totally missing the truth that God was leading this movement from its inception. After presenting this faulty history of our beginnings, the first chapter ends with the reproduction of Ellen White's account of a dream she had when struggling in her spiritual life as a teenager; a dream she had years before the Great Disappointment. He makes few references to that dream throughout the rest of his book, but makes the point that his book is about the fact that we all need to live "Green Cord Dreams." Apparently the author is telling those who read his book that Ellen White's green cord dream was meant to convey the fact that Jesus is all in all; that He is the solution for all our problems; and that we all need "Jesus to be The One" in our lives, apparently the way he believes Ellen White was impressed by that dream.

We have no problem with the fact that Jesus needs to be our all in all, and the center of every aspect of our lives, but that doesn't seem to be the central message of that dream to Ellen White, the one who had the dream.

It is interesting to note that the last sentence of Ellen White's account of that experience, the sentence where Ellen White tells the reader what the dream meant to her, is left out of his book. Here is that omitted, last sentence:

> This dream gave me hope. The green cord represented faith to my mind, and the beauty and simplicity of trusting in God began to dawn upon my soul. (*Life Sketches*, 36)

Apparently to Ellen White that dream was not an ALL Jesus, the One, and only One that we all need and must have to solve all our church's problems. Once again, we don't argue with the truth that Jesus is everything to us, but that was not how Ellen White benefited from that dream. As a teenager, she was struggling with faith and was terribly discouraged. The Lord gave her that dream to encourage her faith. She comments about the dream by saying, "The green cord represented faith to my mind, and the beauty and simplicity of trusting in God began to dawn upon my soul." What began? "The beauty and simplicity of trusting in God." Does this dream represent some dynamic that will solve all the problems in the Seventh-day Adventist Church? No, it does not, and it was never meant to. This is surely the reason why the author did not use it for that purpose in his book. Simply put, he could not use it that way for that was not the meaning of the dream—it did not match his book's theme, where the solutions to our church's problems come from the teachings and beliefs of his apparent heroes, the emergent church teachers and preachers.

Dr. Bryan diligently points out the self-righteousness that exists among some of God's people as well as a testimony concerning statements made at one of the meetings that if Seventh-day Adventists call themselves part of the "remnant church" then they are "arrogant and extremists."

> How silly we look when we tout our church, our religion, and our denomination—when we pose with our holiness and flex our spiritual muscles to show just how righteous we are. When we look into the mirror and admire the body of our own faith tradition—our insights—our brain power—our prophetic or theological prowess; when we brag about our biblical biceps and strut our spiritual stuff.[35]

Concerning his articles, book, and sermons, there is the same emphasis that emergent church leaders share: very little is heard or seen on what would be considered the pillars of our faith.

Sermons:

> Seventh-day Adventist beliefs are rarely presented from the pulpit. The Three Angels' Messages, the Sanctuary message, the Remnant, the distinctive messages of Adventism are not being heard."

While reading the following counsel from the Spirit of Prophecy, consider how he has sought the counsel of the Sunday-keeping emergent churches, whom we are told do not and will not understand the truth because it is sealed up to them.

> But God has given all these truths to His children who are being prepared for the day of God. He has also given them truths that

35 Bryan, *The Green Cord Dream*, 31.

> none of these parties know, neither will they understand. Things which are sealed up to them, the Lord has opened to those who will see and are ready to understand. If God has any new light to communicate, He will let His chosen and beloved understand it, without their going to have their minds enlightened by hearing those who are in darkness and error. (*Early Writings*, 124)

Again we need to read this important statement:

> I was shown the necessity of those who believe that we are having the last message of mercy, being separate from those who are daily imbibing new errors. I saw that neither young nor old should attend their meetings; … If God has delivered us from such darkness and error, we should stand fast in the liberty wherewith He has set us free and rejoice in the truth. God is displeased with us when we go to listen to error, without being obliged to go; … The angels cease their watchful care over us, and we are left to the buffetings of the enemy, to be darkened and weakened by him and the power of his evil angels; and the light around us becomes contaminated with the darkness." (Ibid., 124, 125)

Friends, please reread the quotation above. This is where "darkness" is found, not from the founding of the advent message, but from the meetings where error is mixed with truth. This is counsel that is necessary and valid. Were not the leaders of these movements apathetic to this counsel, at best? Do they not continue to disrespect and neglect it by teaching and proclaiming the emerging church messages, touting and quoting its leaders from our pulpits, and extending invitations for them to preach? Are not these the consequences of following the thinking suggested in *The Green Cord Dream*?

The author suggests that anyone who uses the term "remnant church" is deceived, proud, and arrogant. He counsels us to remove our focus from that which separates us from the other churches, such as prophecy and our unique beliefs, and have open communion with them. This counsel is opposite of what we find in the Spirit of Prophecy:

> And be sure, when you go out to teach others, not to get your minds upon little things, but keep your mind upon the great work of God, for Satan will surely turn you off if possible. Do not try to

be original and get up something you have not heard your brethren speak of, for many have been shipwrecked in this way. Keep the mind upon the third angel's message. When you keep this before the minds of the people, they will see wisdom in it. But when you get a great many little trifling things before them, they become confused just like the Jews. (*Sermons and Talks*, vol. 1, 51)

At this time, when we are so near the end, shall we become so like the world in practice that men may look in vain to find God's denominated people? Shall any man sell our peculiar characteristics as God's chosen people for any advantage the world has to give? Shall the favor of those who transgress the law of God be looked upon as of great value? Shall those whom the Lord has named His people suppose that there is any power higher than the great I AM? Shall we endeavor to blot out the distinguishing points of faith that have made us Seventh-day Adventists? (*Evangelism*, 121)

We are under obligation to declare faithfully the whole counsel of God. We are not to make less prominent the special truths that have separated us from the world, and made us what we are; for they are fraught with eternal interests. God has given us light in regard to the things that are now taking place in the last remnant of time, and with pen and voice we are to proclaim the truth to the world, not in a tame, spiritless way, but in demonstration of the Spirit and power of God." (Ibid.)

Christ has said of His people, "Ye are the light of the world" (Matthew 5:14). We are the Lord's denominated people, to proclaim the truths of heavenly origin. The most solemn, sacred work ever given to mortals is the proclamation of the first, second, and third angels' messages to our world.

Emergent church pastors do not emphasize special truths. They do not know any special truths. The Bible admonishes us that by beholding we are changed. (See 2 Corinthians 3:18) By beholding, by listening to, emergent church pastors, our theology will change to become more and more like theirs.

In a special sense Seventh-day Adventists have been set in the world as watchmen and light-bearers. To them has been entrusted

> the last warning for a perishing world. On them is shining wonderful light from the Word of God. They have been given a work of the most solemn import,—the proclamation of the first, second, and third angels' messages. There is no other work of so great importance. They are to allow nothing else to absorb their attention. (*Evangelism*, 119)

> There is to be no wavering. The trumpet is to give a certain sound. The attention of the people is to be called to the third angel's message. Let not God's servants act like men walking in their sleep, but like men preparing for the coming of Christ." (Ibid.)

Over and over, Inspiration cannot be more clear—give the trumpet a certain sound. How? By preaching our distinctive truths. In this book, you read that all will have to decide with what we judge the truth, Scripture, and the Spirit of Prophecy, or the accusations and attacks of the critics of this book, which will surely arise. Reader—it is your decision.

In chapter 1 of his book, after painting a picture of defeat and failure, the author of *The Green Cord Dream* suggests what we need to do to save our church. He claims that "churches" are no longer the answer. Denominations are out ("When we are so near the end, shall we become so like the world in practice that men may look in vain to find God's denominated people?" *Evangelism*, 121), but spirituality is in, and if we don't climb on board with this new project, discovering the One for ourselves, we'll be left behind and we will lose out on being a part of this grand revival. The claim is made that we must stop acting as if we are God's unique remnant people, and also stop judging others who are in churches that don't believe as we do. He says we need to take the emphasis off of doctrines and prophecy because these things lead to self-righteousness and separate us from the rest of God's people in all these other churches. He claims that we need to treat everyone as brothers and sisters in the Lord, siblings, and that if we don't follow his suggestions, we will need to hang that "going out of business" sign in the window.

In October of 2011, he openly promoted Roman Catholic mystics and contemplative authors at the Adventist Forum on Spiritual Formation at Walla Walla University—authors such as Richard Foster, Dallas Willard, Brennan Manning, and Henri Nouwen. These are not people having "special truths" for our time.

These are authors he has asserted as his "favorites" at that forum meeting; they are also listed on his blog as "must reads." In his Sabbath sermons, he often quotes from leading emerging church leaders and Catholic contemplative authors such as Brennan Manning, and many more. Is this how to "give the trumpet a certain sound?"

How can someone believe in the distinctive teachings of our faith, while at the same time promote authors, teachers, and pastors who are at war with the Ten Commandments and the three angels' messages?

A person who believes in spreading the message of teachers and spiritual leaders like Richard Foster, Dallas Willard, Brennan Manning, and Henri Nouwen, cannot at the same time understand the seriousness of all the counsel from the Spirit of Prophecy quoted above. The two convictions cannot coexist. Those of us who understand our unique calling and mission are abhorred by what these teachers proclaim, and it is likely that anyone who would support their teachings and recommend their books for spiritual guidance simply does not comprehend the calling and mission of the Seventh-day Adventist Church.

When we as Adventists are confronted by those who advocate reading the authors of mysticism, or are preaching and teaching the tenets of mysticism, we should no longer let these errors go without being exposed. We can no longer turn away from them; we must realize that we have the Christian responsibility to be our brother's keeper.

On pages 32 and 33 of *The Green Cord Dream*, the author says, "Adventist Christians must beware of identifying with John the Adventist more than with the One whose advent we preach. We must beware of dwelling on our own prophetic identity more than upon the identity of Jesus Christ." John the Adventist is the one spoken about above from page 31 in *The Green Cord Dream*, who looks into the mirror and admires "the body of our own faith tradition."

The author's problem, above all others, seems to be a failure to see that the identity of Jesus is intimately interwoven with those truths in the three angels' messages. Our prophetic identity is the revelation of our Lord and Savior, Jesus Christ to the world. Jesus cannot be understood or preached without our prophetic identity. I can think of no other way to say it, but I pray that you, the reader, are getting the point—the two are inseparable. It seems likely that this is what is not understood by those who have chosen to go back to Babylon for light, knowledge, and their advanced education and training.

Is what we read above happening? Is it possible they have been "darkened and weakened by him and the power of his evil angels…" and have become "contaminated with darkness" (*Early Writings*, 124). There is no question that they believe in, and are preaching, the Roman Catholic gospel, most likely learned directly from spiritualist teachers at the school they attended, George Fox University, and from the books they are promoting and reading. Their attendance at that school, violating the counsel noted above, and focusing their education on subjects of Roman Catholic origin, may have led to their deception.

The doctrine contained in the three angels' messages defines who God is, what He is like, the plan of salvation, righteousness by faith, and the duty of every true believer until Jesus comes to take us home. To not preach the distinctive truths is to have fallen into the hands of the archenemy of God, who is doing all he can to prevent the true gospel from being preached to the world.

Here is the final point we need to think about. The author has painted a sad picture of our church in his book, and has then made many suggestions of what we need to do to correct everything. The impression is given that we will find in his book some suggestions from the Spirit of Prophecy, from the person God chose to be the messenger of the Lord to His remnant church.

Therein is the point—and the problem. In all the suggestions he gives in order to change the sad picture he constructed of our church and how to solve its problems, we see little or no use of the Spirit of Prophecy. Never does he refer to Inspiration to answer any of the problems that he says we have. He uses the Spirit of Prophecy here and there to promote the idea that Ellen White supports his "Jesus is the One" movement, which is extremely easy to do considering how much Ellen White talks about Jesus, but when it comes to seeking her counsel to solve problems that will arise in the remnant church near the end of time—problems she tackles with practical advice, which in truth involve the very deceptions presented by his book—her counsel isn't there. In his book, papers, articles, teachings, and sermons, the counsel in this area of our unique, inspired prophet is hardly found, much less referred to, with authority.

However, what is found are his own radical, revolutionary opinions, teachings from the churches Adventists consider Babylon, George Fox University, Dr. Leonard Sweet, Richard Foster, Dallas Willard, Brennan Manning, Henri Nouwen, Shane Clairborne, and a list of other mystics and spiritualists, who believe as he believes; types of speakers and authors we are warned against even listening to.

Dr. Bryan has cunningly defined a spiritual problem and then presented it as a straw man, blaming its creation on historic Adventism. He then cleverly suggests ways to get rid of it, especially to the youth. He directs them to the writings of the radical emerging church leaders, whose teachings naturally appeal to them. He expresses those thoughts in both *The Green Cord Dream* and in the article he wrote for *Adventist Today* in 2009. He erroneously defines the problems in the church, and then suggests emergent church solutions, based on the teachings of spiritualists and mystics. He recommends that we read these authors, but is reluctant to seek God's counsel in the Spirit of Prophecy. To summarize:

The Green Cord Dream contains little counsel from the inspired writings contained in the Spirit of Prophecy on how to solve these invented problems. All the suggestions for a cure to the church's problems are from emergent teachers. This is a part of the deception of which every reader needs to be aware.

He believes our church has alienated and separated itself from the world, and counsels us to not be so bold in preaching our distinctive truths, the very truths that define the heart and soul of our movement, truths that motivate every faithful Seventh-day Adventist. I pray that as we conclude *Meet It* with the next few remarks you will see the contradiction of Dr. Bryan's convictions to not be so bold in preaching our distinctive truths, truths that he would like to replace with emergent church teachings.

So, in conclusion, our prophetic identity defines our mission and is intimately interwoven with the person and identity of Jesus. He personifies the three angels' messages. To proclaim this message along with the distinctive truths embodied within it is to preach Jesus, the real "One." It is impossible to separate them. Since the Jesus preached by those in The One Project is lacking these distinctive truths, one could rightfully ask, is the "one" they and the emerging church preach the real Jesus? Impossible! Here's why: The distinctive truths define the most solemn message ever given by mortals and contain the words of Jesus that express His love and set us free. Without the distinctive truths, any message can only contain what Ellen White called a counterfeit "love."

> I have seen the results of these fanciful views of God, *in apostasy, spiritualism, freelovism.* The *free love tendencies* of these teachings were so concealed that it was difficult to present them in their real character. (*Manuscript Releases*, vol. 8, 304, emphasis added)

The "distinctive truths" are words in which are personified the mission and way of salvation—the real Jesus and His real love.

Epilogue

1.

There have been questions raised concerning the exact title and nature of Dr. Bryan's degree from George Fox University.

Whenever an inquiry is made, there is never a reference to the fact that he has a degree in "Leadership and the Emerging Culture," always claiming it is in "Leadership" or "Ministry," or as Alex has said, "Church Leadership and not spiritual practice."

Here is a recent announcement concerning his call to accept the presidency of Kettering. It is the last paragraph of the announcement:

> "Bryan graduated from Southern Adventist University in 1993 with majors in history and religion. He then earned his Master of Divinity from Andrews University in 1996, and his **doctoral degree in ministry from George Fox University in 2009.** He serves as co-chair and presenter for The One Project, a movement celebrating the supremacy of Jesus Christ in the Seventh-day Adventist Church. He also is author of *The Green Cord Dream*, which explores the purpose and possibility for Adventist Christianity in the twenty-first century. He and Nicole have two children, Audrey and William."

We simply want to clarify a simple truth—His degree is in **"Leadership and the Emerging Culture."** The title of this degree has recently changed to Semiotics and Future Studies.

Byran's dissertation is titled "The Role of Human Emotion in Christian Discipleship." While at George Fox Univeristy, he and other The One Project leaders have been involved with the "Leadership and Emerging

Culture" doctor of ministry track, including Semiotics and Future Studies program with Dr. Leonard Sweet.

This track of study:

> "... prepares an advance guard of Jesus semioticians, leaders adept at seeing signs of Jesus' work in the world. These followers of Jesus are not afraid of the future but are excited about its possibilities and promises, while aware of its perils and pitfalls.
>
> The approach is an ancient-future one of MRI (Missional, Relational, Incarnational) discipleship, using an EPIC (Experiential, Participatory, Image-Rich, Connective) interface. Students explore how to transition the church from its current default of APC (Attractional, Propositional, Colonial) to MRI, and play with a variety of EPIC interfaces." (http://www.georgefox.edu/seminary/programs/dmin-sfs/index.html)

Why leave out the main subject for which he received his doctoral degree, "Emerging Culture"? This is according to the records at George Fox University, and is surely written out on the degree itself? See below:

THE FOLLOWING LIST OF GRADUATES FOR 2009 IN DOCTOR OF MINISTRY, WAS RECEIVED FROM THE UNIVERSITY BY REQUEST:

GEORGE FOX UNIVERSITY
OREGON'S NATIONALLY RECOGNIZED *CHRISTIAN* UNIVERSITY

- **ABOUT**
- **ACADEMICS**
- **ADMISSIONS**
- **ATHLETICS**
- **GIVING**
- **RESOURCES**

Marketing Communications
Graduates 2009
City: AK CA DE GA KS MT TN UT VA WI INTL

Tennessee	**Bryan, William Alexander**	**Doctor of Ministry in "Leadership and Emerging Culture"**
California	**Swenson, Terry Robert**	**Doctor of Ministry in "Leadership and Emerging Culture"**

2.

The following are excerpts from *The Green Cord Dream* and from Dr. Bryan's "Rebuttal" letter, where he gave explanations of his statements. The responses are primarily from the author of this book.

GCD, page 85, pp. 4
"God—as pure, intense, radiant light—determines to create. So He makes time, matter, height, depth, animals, minerals, and above all, human beings. And since God is light, life, love, the creatures He makes are filled with light, life and love."

Panentheism (from the Greek), is a belief system which posits that the divine exists (be it monotheistic God, polytheistic gods, or an eternal cosmic animating force), interpenetrates every part of nature and timelessly extends beyond it. Panentheism teaches that God is actually in everything that exists, everywhere. Panentheism was an integral component of the ALPHA and was prophesied to appear again as part of the OMEGA at the end of time.

Rebuttal of Alex Bryan

"I am absolutely opposed to any form of Eastern mysticism..."

GCD page 113, pp 2-3

"The body"

"A vibrant, prevailing, twenty-first century Adventism must paint a compelling and pleasurable picture of the human body

and our experience. We must be well maintained, but we also must be well traveled. Worshipping God with our bodies is about pleasure and experiencing physicality. Creationists believe God created human flesh. The body is good. And just to prove it God came down in the person of Jesus. In human flesh."

Response

Is this concept of the body the one we find in scripture and the Spirit of Prophecy? Are we taught that "**worshiping God with our bodies is about pleasure and experiencing physicality?**" The author's statement that "**The body is good. And that to prove it God came down in person of Jesus,**" is just not correct. Jesus came down to save the human race, not to prove that "**the body is good.**"

Rebuttal Letter:

"I am strongly committed to the life, ministry, and writings of Ellen G. White. My recent book, *The Green Cord Dream*, is a testament to this conviction, as is the ONE project ..."

Ellen G. White

GCD, page 22, pp 2

"In 1842, during this era of Advent hope, fifteen year old, Ellen White had a mystical experience."

Response

By labeling Ellen White a mystic, the author belittles her calling by God as a messenger of the lord with the gift of prophecy. This gives the impression that Ellen White was what the world considers a "mystic." In his book *The Green Cord Dream*, the author chose to recommend very little of Ellen White's counsel, but recommended many authors who are mystics, emerging church leaders, spiritualists, and advocates of spiritual formation, as this book has pointed out.

Ellen G. White

GCD, page 48, pp 4

"Some Adventists deify Ellen White. Others demonize her. Some want to build a shrine in her honor, and others want to burn her books. I have grown to appreciate this woman as neither god nor goddess, but good. She was neither deity nor demon, but a delight. In fact, I have found her to be inspirational."

Response

The author says, "In fact, I have found her to be inspirational." Without qualifying the term "inspirational" with "inspired" or falling within her calling as messenger of the Lord with the prophetic gift, I find this statement to border on heresy. The author has chosen to straddle the fence, choosing to marginalize Ellen White by calling her a "delight." Is that all she is to you, my Adventist brother and sister? Yet nowhere in the GCD does he affirm her to be a prophet of God. "...The testimony of Jesus is the spirit of prophecy." Rev. 19:10 (KJV)

Rebuttal of Alex Bryan

"My use of books written by non-Seventh-day Adventist authors, also, in no way suggests that I agree with everything written therein. Indeed, all Seventh-day Adventists schools of theology utilize books, including our seminary. I critically read and scrutinize all material to comport with the fundamental briefs of the Seventh-day Church."

From *Meet It*, p. 90

The author has fallen into the trap that all who study these books for spiritual growth, or believe they may find some light therein, fall into. It is one thing to read material from the authors of the fallen churches for research and other kinds of analysis, but is a violation of God's counsel to read it with the belief that you can separate the truth from the error and discover the light it contains. From what has been written in *The Green Cord Dream*, the author has obviously accepted many teachings that do not “comport with the fundamental beliefs of the Seventh-day Adventist Church.”

> “Suffer not yourselves to open the lids of a book that is questionable. There is a hellish fascination in the literature of Satan. It is the powerful battery by which he tears down a simple religious faith. Never feel that you are strong enough to read infidel books; for they contain a poison like that of asps. They can do you no good, and will assuredly do you harm. In reading them, you are inhaling the miasmas of hell.” (*Fundamentals of Christian Education*, 93)

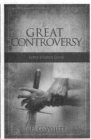

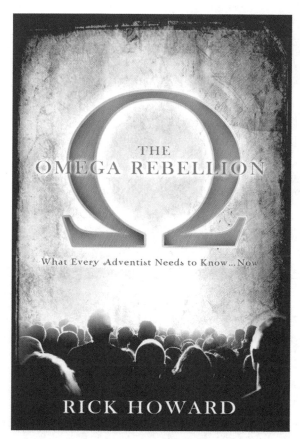

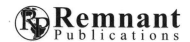